Y0-AFJ-661

MORAL LEARNING

MORAL LEARNING

Some Findings, Issues and Questions

by
Edmund V. Sullivan

in collaboration with
Clive Beck, Maureen Joy
and Susan Pagliuso

PAULIST PRESS
New York / Paramus / Toronto

Library of Congress
Catalog Card Number: 74-31726

ISBN: 0-8091-1872-6

Published by Paulist Press
Editorial Office: 1865 Broadway, N.Y., N.Y. 10023
Editorial Office: 400 Sette Drive, Paramus, N.J. 07652

Printed and bound in the
United States of America

Contents

IN FOND MEMORY OF

GERALD SULLIVAN

ACKNOWLEDGMENTS

We gratefully acknowledge the cooperation of the York County Board of Education and the Ontario Institute for Studies in Education. We wish to express our sincere thanks to the following individuals who have assisted our work: Brian Burnham, Erwin Biener, Robert Czerny, Fahreid Ohan, Margaret Webster, Margaret Liswood, Ronald Wideman, Jacques DuPort, Mary Francis, Nancy Taylor, Nancy Porter, Mary Perri and Pat O'Conner.

We also wish to thank the following schools for their cooperation: Meadowbrook, Prince Charles, Stuart Scott, Whitchurch, Notre Dame, Alderwood, Pickering, Ecole Secondaire Therieault, St. Leonard, Annunciation.

I
Introduction

The aim of this short volume is to present some results of our moral education project which come from the accumulation of four years of work in this area. More specifically, our objective is to attempt to partially integrate several aspects of this project in order to focus on certain issues and questions which our findings, at present, appear to generate. The reader should not expect an exhaustive coverage of issues here since this is not our aim. We will also make some assumptions concerning the type of reader interested in this work. It is expected that the reader has already done some background reading in the area of moral education. Thus, we will not be engaged in the difficult task of attempting to define the domain of moral education both theoretically and practically. Readers interested in this should consult other sources (e.g., Beck, Crittenden and Sullivan, 1971; Wilson, Williams and Sugarman, 1967). A second assumption concerning the reader is that he has some interest in moral education which goes from theory into practice. A considerable amount of theoretical forethought has guided this project and this will be apparent in the historical development of our work (to be discussed shortly). Keeping the above consideration in mind, we would expect our audience to span such professions as curriculum specialists, psychologists, philosophers, and teachers whose specialties bring them into contact with moral and ethical issues. Across this spectrum we would not be surprised to find such areas as religious education, history, social studies, etc. To get a glimpse of the scope of this project we turn to a brief reflection on its history.

HISTORICAL BACKGROUND OF THE MORAL EDUCATION PROJECT

The Charter of the *Ontario Institute for Studies in Education* (OISE) stresses the importance of research, development, and graduate instruction in education for the continuous improvement of educational institutions in the province of Ontario. To this end the Ontario Institute was founded to bring together scholars from all over the world across a variety of disciplines. The beginnings of our own project started rather informally as a result of several small seminars on the general topic of education and values which brought members of the Departments of Applied Psychology and History and Philosophy of Education together. From its outset the project has been interdisciplinary. As our informal seminars continued some broad problem areas emerged. A decision was made to hold a conference on moral education which would center on some of these problem areas. To this end, distinguished scholars from several different fields (eg., philosophy, psychology, sociology, etc.) were invited to the Ontario Institute to address themselves to some of the questions that arose in our informal seminars. The proceedings of this conference were published by the University of Toronto Press, under the title "Moral Education: Interdisciplinary Approaches" (Beck, Crittenden and Sullivan, 1971).

Without casting the slightest doubt on the excellent scholarship which was evident in all the papers prepared for this conference (see Beck et al, 1971), it is nevertheless not too impertinent to say that the paper delivered by Kohlberg set the tone for this conference. As evident from the proceedings, one way or another the discussions kept coming back to this paper.

The work of Lawrence Kohlberg (Kohlberg, 1971) is a sophisticated extension of the pioneering work of Piaget into the area of moral reasoning in children. Unlike Piaget, whose research is based on the young child, Kohlberg's normative model is derived from late elementary school students to adults. His theoretical viewpoint goes under the name of a cognitive-developmental theory of morality. In his initial research in the area of moral judgment he presented students with 10 moral dilemma situations and asked them to judge the morality of the conduct described in the stories. The following is an illustration of the conflict stories presented for evaluation:

> In Europe, a woman was near death from a special kind of cancer. There was one drug that the doctors thought might save her; it was a form of radium that a druggist in the same town had recently discovered. The drug was expensive to make, but the druggist was charging ten times what the drug cost him to make. He paid $200 for the radium and charged $2000 for a small dose of the drug. The sick woman's husband, Heinz, went to everyone he knew to borrow the money, but he could only get together about $1000 which is half of what it cost. He told the druggist that his wife was dying and asked him to sell it cheaper or let him pay later. But the druggist said, 'No, I discovered the drug and I'm going to make money from it.' So Heinz got desperate and broke into the man's store to steal the drug for his wife. Should Heinz have done that? Was it actually wrong or right? Why?

Kohlberg identified six stages in the development of moral judgment, and to some extent these stages are his description of different types of moral character. There are three levels of morality that encompass the six stages. The lower stages are seen in the lower and middle elementary school years, while the middle stages are seen in most high school students with a smattering of the later stages in the later high school years. Kohlberg's (1971) stages and levels of moral maturity are described briefly as follows:

I. *Preconventional level*

At this level the child is responsive to cultural rules and labels of good and bad, right and wrong, but interprets these labels in terms of either the physical or the hedonistic consequences of action (punishment, reward, exchange of favors), or in terms of the physical power of those who enunciate the rules and labels. This level is divided into the following two stages.

Stage 1: The punishment and obedience orientation. The physical consequences of action determine the goodness or badness of an act regardless of the human meaning or value of these consequences. Avoidance of punishment and unquestioning deference to power are valued in their own right, not in terms of respect for an underlying moral order supported by punishment and authority (the latter being stage 4). For example, a stage 1 response to the Heinz dilemma is that Heinz should steal the drug because, "If you let your wife die, you will get into trouble. You'll be blamed for not spending the money to save her, and there'll be an investigation of you for your wife's death." In this example, the respondent would act only out of fear of punishment to himself. Or similarly, "You shouldn't steal the drug, because you'll get caught and be sent to jail if you do." Again, there is no internalized sense of right or wrong—only a fear of consequences.

Stage 2: The instrumental relativist orientation. Right action consists of that which instrumentally satisfies one's own needs and occasionally the needs of others. Human relations are viewed in terms like those of the market place. Elements of fairness, of reciprocity, and of equal sharing are present, but they are always interpreted in a physical pragmatic way. Reciprocity is a matter of "You scratch my back and I'll scratch yours," not of loyalty, gratitude, or justice. For example, "If you do happen to get caught you could give the drug back and you wouldn't get much of a sentence. It wouldn't bother you much to serve a jail term if you have your wife when you get out." Or, "He may not get much of a jail term if he steals the drug, but his wife will probably die before he gets out so it won't do much good." The stage 2 respondent has no moral commitment, and would act in terms of personal pleasure only.

II. *Conventional level*

At this level, maintaining the expectations of the individual's family, group, or nation is perceived as valuable in its own right, regardless of immediate and obvious consequences. The attitude is not only one of *conformity* to personal expectations and social order, but of loyalty to it, of actively *maintaining*, supporting and justifying the order, and of identifying with the persons or group involved in it. At this level, there are the following two stages.

Stage 3: The interpersonal concordance of "good boy—nice girl" orientation. Good behavior is that which pleases or helps others and is approved by them. There is much conformity to stereotypical images of what is majority or "natural" behavior. Behavior is frequently judged by intention—"he means well" becomes important for the first time. One earns approval by being "nice". Examples of stage 3 responses are as follows: "No one will think you're bad if you steal the drug but your family will think you're an inhuman husband if you don't. If you let your wife die you'll never be able to look anybody in the face again." Or, "It isn't only the druggist who will think that you're a criminal—

everyone else will too. If you steal knowing that, you'll dishonor your family and yourself."

Stage 4: The "law and order" orientation. There is orientation toward authority, fixed rules, and the maintenance of the social order. Right behavior consists of doing one's duty, showing respect for authority, and maintaining the given social order for its own sake. For example, "If Heinz steals the drug, he will set an example that could cause anarchy and the destruction of more lives than his wife." "If you have a sense of honor, you won't let your wife die. You'll always feel guilty that you caused her death, if you don't do your duty to her."

III. *Postconventional, autonomous, or principled level*

At this level, there is a clear effort to define moral values and principles which have validity and application apart from the authority of the groups or persons holding these principles, and apart from the individual's own identification with these groups. This level again has two stages.

Stage 5: The social-contract legalistic orientation. Generally with utilitarian overtones. Right action tends to be defined in terms of general individual rights, and standards which have been critically examined and agreed upon by the whole society. There is a clear awareness of the relativism of personal values and opinions and a corresponding emphasis upon procedural rules for reaching consensus. Aside from what is constitutionally and democratically agreed upon, the right is a matter of personal "values" and "opinion". The result is an emphasis upon the "legal point of view", but with an emphasis upon the possibility of changing law in terms of rational considerations of social utility (rather than freezing it in terms of stage 4 "law and order"). Outside the legal realm, free agreement and contract is the binding element of obligation. For example, "Although Heinz would be breaking the law to steal the drug, what good is the law if it prevents his wife from living. The druggist's actions are totally immoral, and Heinz has no choice but to steal the drug."

Stage 6: The universal ethical principle orientation. Right is defined by the decision of conscience in accord with self-chosen *ethical principles* appealing to logical comprehensiveness, universality, and consistency. These principles are abstract and ethical (the Golden Rule, the categorical imperative); they are not concrete moral rules like the Ten Commandments. At heart, these are universal principles of *justice*, of the *reciprocity* and *equality* of human *rights*, and of respect for the dignity of human beings as *in-*

dividual persons. For example, "Heinz must steal the drug if his actions are to save a human life. A law that permits his wife to die is an immoral one, because it violates the universal principle that everyone has an equal right to life. Heinz must disobey this law because it is incompatible with the well-being of mankind."

Kohlberg's theory is labelled as cognitive-developmental because its emphasis is on the judgmental or reasoning aspects of a moral situation (i.e., cognitive) and the theory, backed by empirical data postulates that the development of moral judgment follows an invariant pattern of levels and stages from childhood through adulthood (i.e., developmental). We will present normative data related to this theory in Chapter 2.

Stage Development and Transition. Although Kohlberg's stage theory postulates an invariant stage sequence he does not mean to indicate that the highest stages will be reached without specific types of environmental experiences. In fact, moral stage development in our culture tends to peak out at the level of conventional morality. Stage development in Kohlberg's theory is said to result from cognitive conflict produced by certain kinds of environmental stimulation interacting with the particular stage of the individual. The cognitive conflict is said to be optimal for development when the environmental input is one level above the person's present stage. A colleague of Kohlberg's, working with sixth grade children, demonstrated that messages one stage above their own were assimilated and subsequently used to a greater extent than were messages two stages above or one stage below their present stage of development. Subsequent studies completed by Kohlberg and colleagues have given support to these findings.

According to Kohlberg, the developmental and experimental findings suggest a coherent philosophic and psychological approach to moral education. One assumption here is that moral development passes through a *natural* sequence of stages. The approach defines the aim of moral education as stimulation of the next step in the natural development of the child, rather than indocrination into the fixed conventions of the school, the church, or the nation. A further assumption is that movement to the next step of development rests not only on exposure to the next level of

thought, but experience of conflict in the person's application of
his current level of thought in problematic situations.

The Hidden-Curriculum. Kohlberg (1971) maintains that the
school, by its very nature, is involved in the process of moral values. Any attempt to deny the fact that morality is endemic to
schooling is an indication that the institution of the school refuses
to make explicit some elements of the curriculum. When moral
values are not explicit they are said to be operating in the school in
a *hidden-curriculum.*

> The term 'hidden-curriculum,' then, refers to the fact that
> teachers and schools are engaged in moral education without
> explicitly and philosophically discussing or formulating its
> goals and methods (Kohlberg, 1971 in Beck, Crittenden and
> Sullivan, pp 29-30).

In general, the school seems geared to the inculcation of values
which are at Kohlberg's level 3 (i.e., conventional level). Kohlberg
maintains that the unreflective moral education in the hidden-curriculum reflects the unconscious wisdom of society and its needs
for "socializing" the child for his own welfare.

Mackay Commission Report

Our reason for dwelling on Kohlberg's theory at this point is
because of the influence that his paper played in the formulation of
the Mackay Commission Report. The formal title of this report
was "Religious Information and Moral Development: The Report
of the Committee on Religious Education in the Public Schools of
the Province of Ontario (1969)." Some of the conclusions and di-
rections of this report reflect some of the proceedings of the moral
development conference and this is recognized in the following
quote:

> We note that those scholars who have undertaken the most
> extensive research in moral development in recent years have
> often come to conclusions which are sharply contradictory.
> Perhaps we should not be too surprised that the lay public is
> so often confused about this subject in view of the notable
> lack of inter-disciplinary communication concerning it among

psychologists, philosophers, theologians, sociologists and other investigators. But in this regard we note that in June 1968, the Departments of Applied Psychology and of History and Philosophy of Education in the Ontario Institute for Studies in Education brought together a number of leading international authorities in several unrelated fields in a conference whose topic was "Moral Education: An Interdisciplinary Discussion of Selected Questions." We recommend both the spirit and the vision behind this project, whose reported discussion we ourselves found most valuable, and we express the hope that the subject will continue to be explored seriously by educationists in such ways as this (Mackay Report, p. 41).

The Mackay Committee Report recommended that contemporary education in Ontario needs more "reflective" programs and curricula if the school accepts its responsibility to prepare students to cope in a society in which many social institutions are being questioned and changed.

Specifically when discussing moral education the report clearly shows the influence of Kohlberg's views when it equates character development with the ability to reason morally. Morality is defined as primarily a measure of the student's ability to make moral judgments, and to arrive at decisions on the basis of moral principles. Without taking a critical attitude here in relation to the report's use of Kohlberg's theory, it is quite clear that their conclusions in this area are strongly influenced by his views. The following quote is illustrative:

It should by now be apparent that we believe that the primary concern of moral education should be to stimulate the development of the young person's powers to make value judgments and moral decisions, and that its least important purpose is to teach fixed virtues. Opportunities to make value judgments should therefore be recognized by the student, and he should be sensitized to his responsibility for making them (pp 58-59).

The most important aspect of this report in relation to our project is the kind of atmosphere that it has created for doing work in this area. Some of their recommendations have clearly had a salutary effect on our work since they have encouraged explorations into the school's role in the moral development of the child. For example:

> The curriculum innovation which we recommend, then, in the field of moral education is the establishment of a program (as opposed to a course), to be carefully planned but administered incidentally throughout the whole school spectrum. The program will have as its focus character building, ethics, social attitudes, and moral values and principles—the precise concerns enumerated in our terms of reference. We shall hereafter refer to it as the *moral development program*. Let us repeat that what we are recommending is a program of emphasis throughout the school, not a course of study in a subject area (pp 53-54).

And finally:

> There is little question in our minds that the program we are proposing, and particularly the discussion technique through which moral development of the individual is to be stimulated, will require development and amplification beyond this report. We have not sought to reflect here more than a few of the basic principles of recent developmental theory concerning moral education, although we have endeavored to show how those principles can be applied in the curriculum. . . . But if more is to be discovered concerning the nature of moral development, continued investigation and writing by research persons must be encouraged. We hope that the leadership here will come from qualified scholars in psychology, sociology, philosophy, and related fields (p. 69).

THE CONTEXT OF THE MORAL DEVELOPMENT PROJECT

The most important outcome of the Mackay report, from our point of view, is the favorable atmosphere that it created in Ontario for educational research and development in this complex and controversial area. This encouraging atmosphere was an incentive for several of us to abandon our ivory towers and take on teaching roles in the schools on an experimental basis. Initially, we ran discussion classes in several high schools and then switched some of our efforts into the elementary school years. The project has been in progress for four years and our work has been channelled into a variety of areas which have potential implications for areas of the curriculum where moral or ethical issues may be embedded. The present work is an attempt to summarize some of these initial efforts and ultimately to raise issues and questions that this type of project generates for people interested in the topic of moral education. The following topic headings will be discussed in detail in separate sections: a) Normative Data on Stages of Moral Reasoning, b) Moral Education in the Elementary Schools, c) Moral Education in the Secondary Schools, d) Initial Teacher Training Efforts in the Area of Moral Education, and e) Retrospect and Prospect: Issues and Questions Generated by the Project.

II
Normative Data on
Stages of Moral Reasoning

Most of our early efforts on this project were directed toward accumulating information about how children and adolescents reason on moral problems. This early interest led us naturally into looking at the work of Piaget and Kohlberg since their research was directly related to the investigation of moral reasoning. Kohlberg's stage theory of moral reasoning intrigued us for both theoretical and applied reasons. Although we did not share all of Kohlberg's views on the definition of morality, we nevertheless shared his interest in the development of moral reasoning as a very important focus for the schools. We also partially shared with Kohlberg, the emphasis on the development of moral reasoning as a viable objective for the schools to pursue. As educators, we were interested in the intellectual framework of moral reasoning, even independent from moral action. In other words, we felt that moral reasoning was an intellectual activity which has relevance in a school setting and regardless as to whether its ultimate outcome results in the practice of virtue, it still can be considered an important activity as a prerequisite for the practice of virtue. Here our argument is in line with Dewey who called for a more serious consideration of moral principles in the educational process:

> We have associated the term ethical with certain special acts which are labeled virtues and are set off from the mass of other acts. . . . Moral instruction is thus associated with teaching about these particular virtues, or with instilling cer-

tain sentiments in regard to them. The moral has been con-
ceived in too goody-goody a way. Ultimate moral motives and
forces are nothing more or less than social intelligence. . . .
There is no fact which throws light upon the constitution of
society, there is no power whose training adds to social re-
sourcefulness that is not moral (Dewey, 1959, p. 42-43).

Dewey lamented the separation of intellectual and moral
training, since it was indicative of a failure to conceive of the
school as a social institution with responsibility for character and
moral education. In *Democracy and Education* (1916), Dewey
made note of a paradox that often accompanies discussion of
morals. On the one hand, morality is identified with rationality,
where reason is the faculty for critical deliberation on moral
choices. On the other hand, morality is often thought of as an area
in which ordinary knowledge and intellectual skills have no place.
Dewey saw this separation as having a special significance for
moral education in the schools, since, if valid, the acquisition of
knowledge and understanding would be treated as something separate from character development. The ultimate outcome of this
separation might be the reduction of moral education to a form of
catechetical instruction, or to lessons about morals, an alternative
which ignores a much older tradition. Morality and ethics have
had, historically, a much wider scope and conceptual significance,
going far beyond the delineation of a few choice behaviors or virtues. John Dewey was well aware of this earlier tradition when he
argued for a more serious consideration of moral principles in the
education process.

The intriguing aspect of Kohlberg is that his theory attempts
to empirically specify developmental stages in moral reasoning.
Kohlberg's research is largely an outgrowth of Piaget's pioneering
work in the field.

Piaget (1932) presented children with a series of paired stories
centering on a moral issue and asked the children to make judgments as to the naughtier action and the extent of culpability. The
following is an example:

a) There was once a little girl who was called Marie. She
wanted to give her mother a nice surprise, and cut out a piece of

sewing for her. But she didn't know how to use the scissors properly and cut a big hole in her dress.

b) A little girl called Margaret went and took her mother's scissors one day when her mother was out. She played with them for a bit, and then, as she didn't know how to use them properly, cut a little hole in her dress. Who is the naughtier of the two children?

Younger children judged Marie the naughtier child because she had done the most damage, whereas older children judged Margaret naughtier because of her intentions. On the basis of these age differences in response to this and other stories, Piaget formulated a two-stage theory of moral development. A heteronomous (objective) stage (approximately four to eight years) is based on an ethic of authority. The child views moral rules and restraints as laid down from above. Rules have a literal interpretation, are sacred, and cannot be changed. An act is morally wrong because it is defined in terms of adult sanctions (i.e., an act is wrong if it is punished by an adult). The child believes in "imminent justice" in which the punishment follows invariably upon a violation; its severity varies directly with the magnitude of the consequences of the action, and ignores the motive which inspired it. Because of the child's intellectual limitations, moral rules are considered external (transcendental); this lack of an internalized rule system encourages adherence to external punishment by superordinate adults. Thus, moral duty is simply seen as obedience to adult authority.

Piaget calls the second stage autonomous (subjective) morality (approximately eight years and above). This type of morality is egalitarian and democratic; the child operates on his "own moral rules" inspired by mutual respect and cooperation with others. Piaget (1932, 1951) maintains that autonomous morality arises from the child's interaction with his peers. The movement away from unilateral respect for adults and the increasing development of mutual respect and solidarity with peers helps the child realize that rules are compacts, arrived at and maintained by equals, in the common interest. Rules are no longer sacred and can be changed by mutual consent and in extenuating circumstances. Punishment is not an absolute necessity and, in place of being expiatory, it is now specific to the infraction. Moreover, punishment is guided by a principle of equity which takes into consideration the motive underlying the act and the circumstances under which the transgression was committed.

Kohlberg's (1971) work is a more sophisticated extension of Piaget. Unlike Piaget, whose research is based on the young child, Kohlberg's normative model is derived from late elementary school students to adults. He claims that the forms of reasoning are universal to all cultures and he cites cross-cultural evidence which indicates that his developmental stages follow the same invariant stage sequence in such cultures as the U.S., India, Martinique, etc. (Kohlberg, 1971). In all of these cultures one finds that younger children initially perceive rules and expectations as external to the self (Level I); the self is identified or equated with the rules, stereotypes, and expectations of others (Level II); and finally, the self is differentiated from conventional rules (Level III).

Canadian Norms

Our initial interest in Kohlberg's theory made us sensitive to the fact that his initial norms might be culture bound. For both theoretical and practical reasons, we decided it would be helpful to see how Canadian populations compared with the stage norms that Kohlberg had established in the United States.

Our first sample consisted of 120 pupils drawn from three age levels: 12, 14, and 17 years (Sullivan, McCullough, and Stager, 1970). The pupils were of average intelligence with I.Q.'s falling roughly in the 95-125 range of ability. Developmental stages were determined through Kohlberg's moral judgment questionnaire which consisted of nine hypothetical conflict stories with corresponding sets of probing questions concerning such problems as stealing and mercy killing. The developmental trends over age can be seen in Figure 1. The lowest level thinking is most frequent in the 12 year olds whereas the higher level thinking is greatest in the 17 year old group. The 14 year olds are in between the other groups as would be expected. Our trends are similar to those found by Kohlberg.

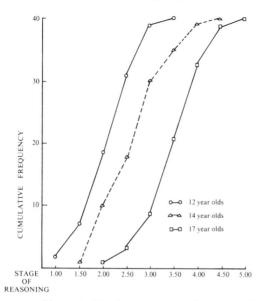

Figure 1. Distribution by age of scores on Kohlberg's
questionnaire (Sullivan, et al, 1970).

In order to give a more specific picture of stage distribution
across ages, we have combined moral judgment stage scores from
a number of both elementary and secondary schools in which we
have worked. The following data combines male and female moral
judgment scores from five elementary schools. Figure 2 is the combined data from these schools over the 9 and 13 age range. The
younger children, that is the 9 and 10 year olds, respond with predominant stage 1 and 2 judgments and a small number of stage 3
responses. There is notably absent from these samples, stage 4, 5
and 6 moral reasoning. At 11 years of age you will note that stage
3 responses are getting stronger and this is most clearly seen in the
12 year old groups where stage 1 responses have fallen off marked-
ly. The 13 year old groups are somewhat oddball, but the trends are
quite similar to the 12 year old group. It is clearly evident in the 9 to
13 year old age range that post-conventional stage 5 and 6 thinking
is absent.

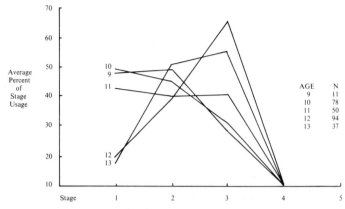

Figure 2. Kohlberg's stages of moral reasoning be-
tween the ages of 9 and 13.
Stage 1: Punishment and obedience orien-
tation.
Stage 2: Instrumental relativism.
Stage 3: "Good boy—nice girl" orienta-
tion.
Stage 4: Law and order orientation.
Stage 5: Social contract legalistic orienta-
tion.
Stage 6: Universalizable moral principles.

Figure 3 is the combined data from three secondary schools
over the 15 through 18 age ranges. Between 15 and 18 years the
trends are essentially the same for all subjects. There is a modal
predominance of stage 3 thinking and the beginning of stage 4 and
5 thinking. The main difference between this age range and the 9
and 12 year olds is the budding presence of post-conventional reasoning (i.e., stage 5). Both figures 2 and 3 present in stage form
the trends seen in figure 1. The importance of this normative data
will become clear when we discuss our initial teaching attempts in
both the elementary and secondary schools. To this we will now
turn.

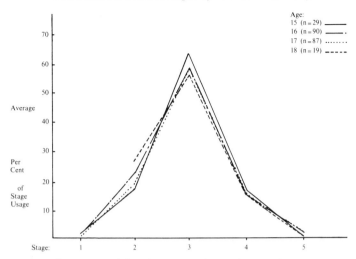

Figure 3. Kohlberg's stages of moral reasoning between the ages of 15 and 18.

III

Moral Education
in the Elementary School

A major consideration in trying our hand at moral education in the elementary school years stemmed from our desire to understand children's thinking on value issues during the middle years of childhood. As already indicated, our normative data indicated a movement from Kohlberg's pre-moral level of thinking to the conventional level during the elementary school years. Our research and development was partly guided by this developmental perspective and at the outset we chose fifth graders with a view to following these students for at least three years. Initially, education officers of a neighboring county encouraged and authorized our work. Assessment of students' moral judgment stage was made in four schools of this county. Two of the project members ran pilot courses in two of the schools. Thus, a central component of our work with the elementary schools has included a research (assessment) and development (teaching) focus. In the second year of the project we were also able to teach classes in two Toronto schools. Our comments on teaching strategies represent a composite of experiences.

Our project proceeded on the assumption that moral education in the elementary schools is a process by which children learn the art and skills of decision making through conflict resolution. In working with elementary school children we were struck by the fact that they were regularly confronted and involved in the moral issues. Indeed, questions of right and fairness emerge as soon as the child can reflect on his role vis-à-vis other persons. Their sense of fair play is obvious not only in early games (Piaget) but in their appeal to equality in family life ("He got more than I did"). The child's understanding of fairness however, is simplistic—but nevertheless it is a valuable and necessary point of departure for gradually developing a sense of complexity and alternatives in human relations.

When quizzed, adults can often remember early experience of moral dilemmas. A researcher in our project describes this early event:

> At about age four, my parents called the children together—my six year old brother Jimmie, the baby, Lucille, two, and myself. They carefully and kindly announced the bad news that since Jimmie had asthma and was allergic to dogs, we would have to send our well loved setter Brian to a farm. I felt badly about Jimmie's asthma but was baffled by the solution. Brian it seemed to me, was perfectly innocent. Jimmie had asthma, why not send Jimmie to the farm?

The child is unable to express such difficulties. Nonetheless he feels that fairness demands a different look at "competing claims." Sympathy and understanding were not adequate approaches to this child. The parents might have tried to have the child talk about the problems, to understand what the child was thinking. The result might have been a discussion of differences between human beings and animals and, hopefully, some help to the child in understanding that it was fair to send Brian to a farm.

As children begin to live in more structured school societies they need and deserve assistance in examining rules, roles and rights of the members of the school community. In fact the school as a miniature society is a powerful resource for the child's introduction into the larger world. The socializing power of the school has long been recognized and has a hidden-agenda which promotes conformity. Following cognitive development theory, the school authority is the main distributor of punishment and reward for conformity and compliance. Indeed one can make the case that the marking system successfully engages the pupil in the system. The school can also encourage fellowship, law and order and lead the student to conventional levels of morality. The school structure, for good or ill, promotes certain standards. More and more frequently older students are rejecting authoritarian style schools. They reject the discipline, arbitrariness and confinement of the school. These older students are in fact discovering the "hidden curriculum". The hidden curriculum for younger children, again for good or ill, is a more powerful force because they are less able to perceive its limitations. Beck (1971) argues for an open curriculum where values, norms, rules are consciouslessly examined and revised for the good of the whole community.

Given the current state of affairs in a progressive province like Ontario, the conditions seemed favorable for the initiation of specific pilot courses for younger children which encouraged reflection on values. As noted above, the climate is favorable in the seventies for a renewed look at the topic of morals and values in the schools. This climate offers opportunity to isolate part of the school program and give direct attention to moral/value issues.

Rationale for Teaching Approaches

Our general criteria for selection of teaching approaches for elementary school students were these:

1) Selection of topics relevant to students' life situation. We have used a contextual rather than an individualistic approach. We sought to deal with issues that ought to be termed "the individual and society." Our work cannot be termed "guidance" or sensitivity training.

2) Selection of topics readily adaptable to different approaches based on the background, interest, concerns of different groups of students.

3) Selection of methods that stimulate cognitive moral development. Initial testing and evidence of other investigators showed that fifth grade students are at a pre-conventional level of moral reasoning. We did not confine ourselves to a single moral dilemma approach. Instead we experimented with a variety of methods—all designed to stimulate analysis, discussion and response to value issues.

4) Selection of methods that would draw on student resources on their own power to help each other work through problems and issues.

These broad criteria reveal a basic concern of the OISE project. Our aim has been one of flexibility and adaptability in learning situations. We decided originally not to package curriculum materials and we continue to feel that such packaging is not necessary. Ample material is available for moral education programs and we have used examples of these materials. From our perspective, we feel that we can best assist teachers in suggesting uses of materials not adding to the quantity already flooding the market. Just as we do not encourage prescriptive morality, so we do not encourage prescriptive approaches to teaching.

A key notion in all of our work with students and teachers is that of "structure". The complexity of value questions, the unease with which both teachers and students begin critical examination of value issues, requires, it seems to us, a clear set of ground rules and boundaries. We have observed free wheeling, non-directed classes, where students become dissatisfied and disenchanted with vagueness and looseness.

Beck's suggestions for a teaching approach that gives students a sense of structure and order is labelled the "principled discussion" method (Beck, 1971). Beck has outlined topics for fifth and sixth graders under the broad heading "Human Relations". For each of the topics he offers a basic principle and guiding questions for the discussion. At first glance this structure seems rigid, but in fact, it allows ideas to be examined within a broad framework. The usefulness of his method is largely a function of teaching style. Teachers who prefer a disciplined (in the best sense of the word) approach to learning how to examine issues find this structure very helpful.

In the second and third years of the project we have worked with teachers who themselves have expanded, modified, provided alternate structures for dealing with "Human Relations". These will be discussed in the section below on specific teaching issues. Those comments will be more useful after a description of the students, teachers and school settings in which we worked.

Description of Students, School Settings

We have introduced programs of moral education into two county schools and two Toronto Schools. Our county work has included yearly assessment of students' level of moral development combined with an experimental teaching program. The Toronto work has focussed primarily on experimental approaches and in-service education of teachers.

The county schools, Elliott and Wansbrough,* are located about forty miles from Toronto. Elliott is a "traditional" school, Wansbrough an "open plan" school. The terms refer to architectural structure. Students in both schools belong to a suburban farm community setting. It is impossible to give the label "middle class" "rural". We did find however that the Elliott classes seemed a clearer unit than classes at Wansbrough. This seems largely due to the fact that Elliott is in the downtown area. All children live close to the school (most within walking distance) and share out of school experiences. Wansbrough is a remote section of a nearby town. Ninety-five percent of the four hundred students are bused to the school.

We selected two city schools, Delamere and Newberry, in the second year of teaching—again one "traditional" school and one "open plan" architecturally. Both schools draw students from middle class residential areas. Again, it is impossible to stereotype the students. The mix is ethnic: Canadian, Chinese, British, Indian children are students in these classes.

It is of real significance that no schools in the elementary aspect of the project are in low income areas. We have had the opportunity to work with teachers in inner city schools and in isolated rural areas. We will comment on their response to our work in a later section.

Teaching Format: Issues and Problems

As noted above we designed mini-courses that would encourage reasoning on value issues. The first year of the project emphasized the "theoretical discussion" method. It was very clearly a deductive approach. The second year might be termed "event study", an inductive approach designed to stimulate involvement, response and unfolding of principles. We use the term "event study" in its broadest sense—current events, hypothetical situa-

---

*All schools involved have been given fictitious names.

tions, personal or school vignettes etc. Both approaches are dynamic in that they require close attention on the part of the teacher to content, structure, pace and range.

Decisions on specific content, structure, pace and range, revolved around maximizing both teacher learning and student learning. A comparison of the two approaches focusing on these four points reveals the advantages of both and broad issues and questions that emerge in elementary school moral education programs.

Theoretical Discussion Method

Beck (1971) sets forth a theoretical mini-course in human relations with the following content topics. Each topic might occupy about two forty-minute periods. 1. Rules people give us. 2. The place of rules in society. 3. Exceptions to society's rules. 4. The individual's need for other people. 5. Helping other people. 6. The self and others. 7. The place of laws, judges, and police. 8. The place of governments and other authorities. 9. Law-breaking and the place of punishment. 10. Different values and rules in our society. 11. Different values and rules around the world. 12. Loyalty and patriotism. 13. The place of the inner group of relatives and friends. 14. Parent-child relationships. 15. Prejudice against races, social classes and other groups. 16. Differences in taste in our society and around the world. 17. Settling conflicts of interest in society. 18. The role of the school in solving society's problems. 19. Students, teachers and schools. 20. The individual and society. 21. Studying society and working out solutions to its problems.

Children were given study notes on each of these topics. They thus had a structure—a sense of direction for the learning session or sessions. The following is a sample of discussion material for the first topic "Rules people give us"!

Principle for Discussion

Rules and principles given to us by other people are not always very good. Often we should take no notice of them at all. Sometimes we should change them a bit to make them better. Sometimes we should make up our own rules.

Possible Examples

1. In some schools, children are given the rule: "Never talk to another child in the classroom." Is this a good rule? Why?

2. In some families children are told: "Never break a promise." What do you think about that rule?

3. Often children are taught by others to follow the rule: "If someone pushes or hits you, always hit him back." Is that a good principle?

4. Some parents tell their children: "Always read what your teacher tells you to read." Do you feel that is right?

5. On television, we might be told: "Always use Nodekay toothpaste." Should we follow this rule?

Some Ideas and Theories

(a) Some people believe that all rules are good. They feel that if there is a rule in society, it must be a good one, because otherwise why is it there? Do you agree with this way of thinking?

(b) It may be, however, that a bad rule is made because of a mistake. For example, in the old days, doctors used to follow the rule of taking blood from people when they were ill so as to make them better. But this was a mistake. In most cases it was the wrong thing to do. Also, in the old days, people used to burn women to death if they thought they were witches. But this, too, was a mistake, as there is no such thing as a witch. Do you think that bad rules are still sometimes made today because of mistakes?

(c) Sometimes, perhaps, bad rules are given to us for self-centered reasons. People want us to do something which is good for *them*; so they persuade us to follow a rule which will help *them*, without really caring about *us*. For example, commercials on television and in the newspaper are often like that. The person who makes the toothpaste or ballpoint pen or chocolate bar may be more concerned with selling his product and making money than with satisfying us. Or again, sometimes when adults give children rules of behavior, they are more concerned with their own comfort and convenience than with the happiness of the children. Of course, adults should look after themselves. But sometimes, perhaps, they go too far. What do you think?

(d) Some people think that it is best to follow all the rules you are given because, although some of them may be bad, it will work out best overall. You get into so much work and trouble trying to make up your own rules, they say, that it is not worth it. It is best just to accept all the rules and principles given to you by your family, church, government, and society. What do you think of this opinion?

Some Further Subjects for Study

1. How many different kinds of rules can you think of (health rules, school rules, etc.) which are given to you by others? Draw up a list of kinds.

2. How many different kinds of people and groups give rules to you? Again make up a list. (This list may contain some of the same items as the first list.)

3. Under each kind of rule (from list 1) find examples (a) of rules which you think are good ones, and (b) of rules which you think are bad ones (if any).

These study notes allow the teacher to follow student pace and to examine a range of issues relating to a topic. Undoubtedly the topics chosen are ones of concern to the teacher. One can see however, that they are designed to raise questions in the student's mind and to give the teacher the opportunity to respond once he perceives the student's own level of understanding. A major feature of the "theoretical discussion approach" is the importance of the teacher taking a strong leader role. A short segment of the class discussing the sample study notes above illustrates this point: *"Compromise" is not a standard term in moral codes. Its importance is not evident to children. You will see that the teacher directs the dialogue:*

TEACHER:	Suppose 2 pioneers both see some good land. What could they do?
D.M.:	They could divide it in half and put up fences.
J.L.:	They could have a fight and whoever won would get the land.
M.E.:	You could kill the other guy.
M.R.:	You could flip a coin for it.

TEACHER:	They could also decide to farm the land *together*. What would be the advantages?
J:L.:	They could split up the chores. If raiders came they could fight them off.
C.P.:	If they needed machinery they could both put up the money and share it.
M.R.:	There would be more room if there was no fence.
TEACHER:	There are many different kinds of compromise. The purpose of morality is to find better and better compromises. Can you think of some other examples of compromise?
B.W.:	If there was a strike at a business they would have to work out a compromise.
K.S.:	What if 2 boys find one ball?
M.R.:	They could play catch?"

The teacher controls both content and line of discussion in the pure theoretic discussion form. Students in a traditional school setting (Elliott) seem to respond more positively than their free school peers at Wansbrough. The approach follows a structure that is more in line with traditional school practice. It was necessary to adapt the method, structure, but not the content for free school students. On the one hand they needed more activity and stimuli—film, role play, etc. to engage their attention, on the other the pace of ideas was slowed down. The free school pupils were not accustomed to the discussion of ideas. The process of engaging them in a new style of thinking was a slow and difficult one.

Event Approach

The importance of responding directly to each group of children became even more evident in the use of the "event approach". Choice of content, in that style, is only broadly specified. Unlike the theoretic discussion approach, we organized a variety of learning activities based on evidence of students' stage of development. We knew from normative data previously discussed, that the sixth grade classes hovered most generally at stages 2 and 3. We therefore highlighted episodes that would stimulate discussion at stages three and four. We also selected structures that would encourage dialogue among peers. Since "mixed" stages existed we felt that peer response was an effective resource available in any group. Whether or not students are more credible to each other than the teacher-authority, we felt that discussion of any question would possibly be more open and free if the importance and legitmacy of student comment and questions were honored.

Thus in the "event approach" attention to structure is central. We used this approach during the second year in Elliott & Wansbrough and in two additional city schools with sixth, seventh and eighth graders (eight different groups of students in all). The first session with each group was instruction in the town meeting method: simple parliamentary rules, rotating chairman's role, etc. Children volunteered at each session for "chairman", "board person". It was the board person's responsibility to put initials of anyone who wanted to speak on the board. We had some fear at first that the town meeting might be too structured. In fact, in six of the eight groups it became highly flexible, it allowed high protection, low risk for all students to participate in discussions. As students gained control of the structure, teacher dominance decreased. The teacher followed rules about name on the board, etc. The teacher had major responsibility for selection of topic—but students were encouraged to set the meeting agenda.

Student response to this method in six of the groups was overwhelmingly positive. Two groups, the country free school (Wansbrough) and one city traditional school (Delamere) responded "poorly" to the method. The free school children needed and wanted even tighter structures. The courtroom examination of events pleased them most. They would arrange the room, select judge, prosecutor, defense, witness, jury. The traditional groups were accustomed to regular, sophisticated discussions. They quickly adapted the town meeting style to a serious debate format.

With all groups current event content was most regularly introduced. At first the teacher controlled this aspect of the work. Gradually students themselves selected events. One that illustrates the range of concerns in this method was a principal-student-parent-board episode that occurred recently in one of the nearby school districts.

Briefly, a principal had strapped seven students without using proper guidelines for the punishment. One parent complained to the board and the principal received notice of suspension the following Tuesday. At the home and school meeting on Wednesday— a majority of parents objected to hasty action by board. They kept children at home in protest of board action. Discussion of this event differed in the schools:

Wansbrough (free school) public trial of the principal—found innocent primarily because of long service to the school. Jury accepted defense argument that he was simply caught tired at the end of a tough week and from all reports was generally a 'nice guy'. A stage 3 orientation in Kohlberg's terms.

Elliott (traditional) town meeting. Focus on parents' decision to keep children home. Vote at the end of the meeting 50-50 supporting parents. Some felt that students might lose their school year (stage 2 arguments), some felt that one week out wouldn't hurt anyone—except perhaps a very weak student.

Newberry (open plan) town meeting. Focus on principal's responsibility. Strong arguments showing sympathy for principal, but finally broad agreement that he had taken the law into his own hands. Approval of strong board action on legal grounds (stage 4 arguments).

In summary the "event study" approach does free the teacher to learn *what* and *how* students are thinking. He or she can use this knowledge to pace and expand student thinking. The event study approach we suggest is both "tighter" and "looser" than the principled discussion approach. In the final analysis teachers will select the one that is most appropriate for their own style, the school environment and the students' needs (see Hunt and Sullivan, 1973).

Assessment of Differences in Moral Reasoning between Experimental and Control Groups

In the fall of 1970 we interviewed students from Elliott (Experimental Group, N = 27) as well as students from McDonald (Control Group, N = 24), a traditional school from a neighboring county. (A detailed analysis was not conducted on the other four schools already mentioned.) The pre-test was given to all the students selected at Elliott and McDonald before the "experimental group" started to work with value issues.* The first post-test was given a full year later and the second post-test or follow-up was given another full year after this (one year after the completion of the course). 21 McDonald students (Control) and 20 Elliott students (Experimental) completed this third moral reasoning questionnaire in October 1972. The questionnaires were scored in order to determine the stage(s) at which each child was thinking.

Statistical analysis of the differences between the two groups at pre, post, and follow-up tests showed the following. First of all, there were no statistically significant differences in stage of reasoning between the experimental and control group on the pre-test. At the end of the first year (Post-test) both McDonald (Control) and Elliott (Experimental) students responded to the test at a significantly higher level than on the initial pre-test. However, there is no significant difference *between* the groups at the end of the first year (post-test). Finally, at the end of the second year both groups of students had responded at an even higher level but the Elliott students had progressed significantly *more* than the McDonald students.

Looking at the results more descriptively, the difference between the group which developed without help (McDonald) and the group which participated in the twice weekly discussions (Elliott) can be seen in Figures 4 and 5. These figures show the percentage of students responding at Stages 1 through 4. The general trend for *both* classes reveals a change from predominantly Stage 1 responses on the Pre-Test to predominately stage 3 on the Post-Test. The differences between the two classes are seen in: (1) The emergence of stage 4 responses in both the Post-Test and Follow-Up for Elliott while *no* stage 4 responses appeared from McDonald; and (2) After the first year Elliott students no longer responded at stage 1 (external authority—avoid punishment) but began thinking more at stages 2 and 3; McDonald students on the other hand did not drop stage 1 thinking as drastically.

These profiles show that the class with no discussions about ethics began, in Grade 5, by responding to dilemmas in terms of

---

*The control group did not explicitly work on value issues.

Control Group

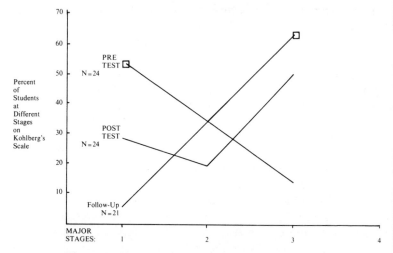

Figure 4. Change in level of major stage from pre-
test to follow-up (Control Group).

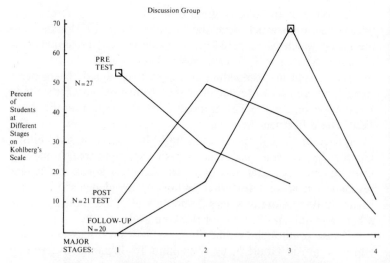

Figure 5. Change in level of major stage from pre-test
to post-test to follow-up (Discussion Group).

obeying authorities (or rules) to avoid punishment or get reward (i.e., Kohlberg's preconventional). At the end of Grade 6 the class had *incorporated* the rules of the authorities and was responding largely on that basis (i.e., conventional). The profile for the class which had discussed ethics begins with the same reliance on external authority. At the end of the first year, however, the students had definitely swung to an orientation in which they began thinking more independently, using ideas of fairness, reciprocity and equal sharing. At the same time a few students began thinking in the larger context of society.

*   *   *   *   *

However supportive educators and the public at large have been to our work we feel that the underlying philosophic premises on which moral education is based require regular review and critical examination. At the outset we had strong hopes for discovering processes for stimulating children to conventional and post-conventional moral reasoning power. Our work has been interpreted as a program which encourages society conformist behavior. In fact, we are encouraging *thinking*, that will lead to an understanding of society's norms—with a view to critically rejecting or accepting them in adulthood. Our study suggests that conventional thinking may be considered an achievement in the elementary school child. Moreover such conventional thinking is the norm for secondary school students. We do not want to underestimate the significance of the child's ability to think conventionally. Such power enables the child to function in current society.

At this point we will not dwell on the possible wider implications of our findings. We will, in our final chapter, provide a more extensive discussion on some issues and questions which the findings of this and other chapters raise.

IV

Moral Education
in the Secondary School

Our work with adolescents in the secondary schools began prior to our elementary school experiences in the fall of 1969 at Campbell High School (see Beck, Sullivan and Taylor, 1972). In fact, our initial pilot work in schools started with the Campbell experience. As in the elementary schools, we utilized Kohlberg's model in order to get a general idea of our students' levels and stages of moral reasoning. The normative data that we have already quoted, indicated that most high school students reason at the conventional level (i.e., stages 3 and 4 of Kohlberg's system) with a dominance of stage 3 thinking. We also noted some stage 2 and 5 orientations. Our focus on moral reasoning may seem to some, onesided. Certainly one aspect of character development that early workers in this field considered important was the demonstrated congruence between a person's evaluative judgments and his conduct (Sullivan and Beck, 1972). A person is said to "have character" if his actions are in keeping with what he judges to be morally good or bad. The earlier character studies done in the 1930's by Hartshorne and May on honesty indicated that children's verbalized knowledge of social standards often disagrees with their behavior when they think they are not being observed. "Talk is cheap and it applies to almost every segment of man's activities". One of the problems we ponder about in our own type of program is the relation of the discussion that goes on in the class with real-life action commitments that might be appropriate outside of the school. In most cases it is virtually impossible to see if moral commitments expressed in the classroom are carried out in extra-curricular settings. At least at the levels of conventional and pre-conventional morality there is room to be skeptical about the realization of expressed thought in actions.

When post-conventional reasoning is being fostered in the classroom is there any reason to expect that there will be a congruence between moral discussion and moral action? The question quite frankly is difficult to answer. We do not know at present just what the relationship might be but can make some conjectures. We suspect that some of our students will become sophisticated talkers and armchair philosophers and even possibly fullfledged academics. This group will have the fiat to talk without tying concrete actions on their convictions. Other post-conventional students will probably become politically active in the university or political party of their choosing and will translate some of their thinking into action. All who continue to question and pursue the reasoning behind conventional rules will have to face some of the alienation that inquiring persons constantly have to face when questioning conventions and rules that are so easily obeyed with blind credulity.

Rationale for Teaching Approaches

Since our aims and objectives are developmental in focus, we proceeded on an assumption that the movement from conventional to the post-conventional levels of maturity represents a more mature "reorganizing, restructuring, and transforming" of the adolescent students' thought processes. In other words, we see the post-conventional level as one that delves into the reasoning behind conventional norms. In this context, Kohlberg's assessment instrument again seems appropriate.

Description of Students and School Settings

Our studies with high school students have been carried out consecutively in two high schools over a period of four years' duration.

The Campbell School. The first classroom discussions were initiated by Clive Beck at Campbell High School. This high school was located in a suburban middle class environment and most of the students and their parents were native born Canadians. These students were planning on a grade 13 option which indicated they are interested in attending university. The class consisted of seventeen students who volunteered to participate in an "experimental" ethics course conducted by Clive Beck, as part of a grade 11 option in the history department of the school. We also had a matched comparison group of students (control group) who were assessed on moral reasoning at various times but who had not attended the "experimental" ethics course. The students in the experimental ethics course met twice weekly for 45 minute classes for a half-semester.

Springdale Collegiate. The students at Springdale were generally lower middle class in background if we consider father occupation. The school was located in one of the suburbs outside of Toronto. Most students were native born Canadians but many of their parents came from several European countries by way of immigration. In general these students did not anticipate a college education and they were in grade 12 at the time of the course. The class was divided equally between boys and girls. It met bi-weekly with Clive Beck and Edmund Sullivan (4 classes a week) for the Fall semester and the off week was devoted to the studies in humanities given by one of the teachers at the school. The Spring semester met bi-weekly for discussion groups with several graduate students who worked with the project. A matched comparison group (control group) were also assessed on moral reasoning but did not take our ethics course.

Teaching Format: Campbell

The class at Campbell extended over a time period of four months. For two forty minute periods a week, a number of topics formed the basis for discussion, although this sequence was not rigidly adhered to, and side topics were introduced occasionally: 1. Some distinctive features of *moral* goodness. 2. Myself and other people. 3. An individual's need for other people. 4. Acting out of moral reasons. 5. The place of mixed motivations. 6. The importance of spontaneity and singlemindedness. 7. The place of moral principles and rules. 8. The value of the act versus the value of the rule. 9. Conscience. 10. Justice, equality and fairness. 11. Developing mutually beneficial solutions. 12. Moral diversity. 13. The pursuit of happiness. 14. An analysis of various virtues and vices.

The course of study was as much an experiment for us as for the students and the school. Our aims and objectives in handling this course were to stimulate moral reasoning at the post-conventional level. We reasoned that discussion and disagreement amongst a group of peers, would produce cognitive conflict in their moral thinking and dissatisfaction with their present perception of moral relationships which was generally at conventional and preconventional levels. Our purpose as educators would be to draw out those ideas which embodied a more mature attitude through asking questions and pointing the way to higher stages of moral thinking. Since most of our class were reasoning at the conventional level (stage 3 and 4) we attempted for the most part to delve into the reasoning behind conventional norms, an understanding which comes with a post-conventional rationale for morality.

The following short summary (taken from the instructor's notes on the class) represents the pattern of a typical discussion and in this case on topic 7 which was concerned with the place of moral principles and rules:

"October 15, 1:35—2:15 p.m.
(The discussion was begun by the instructor)

1. So far we have spent most of our time discussing reasons for following moral principles; I would like us now to turn for a while to the question of *how moral principles come into existence; how and why they are developed.*
   (i) Partly, moral principles are developed in order to avoid fights and general disorder: e.g., the principles of fairness and promise-keeping.
   (ii) Partly, they are developed because they are helpful to most people in a more positive way: e.g., parents teach children to be polite because it is for their own good in the outside world.
   (iii) Partly, as we noted yesterday, they are developed by particular groups to promote their own interests. However, we should not reject moral principles altogether just because we see that they are sometimes used as a kind of trick on other people.

2. Each person must tailor his moral principles to fit his own life;

but this does not necessarily mean that he is rejecting them. Occasionally, a person may indeed have to reject a moral rule altogether, at least in any recognizable form: e.g., a slum child in New York brought up to a gangster life from which he cannot realistically break loose: he may have to reject the rule that it is wrong to steal (although even here the principle may have some value, in relation to his fellow gangsters). On the whole, however, people should not reject moral principles but rather work out what precise form they should take in their own lives individually.

(There was a great deal of disjointed discussion about the notion that each person must tailor his moral principles to fit his own life. Several students expressed misgivings about the idea that it may be morally legitimate for the slum child to steal. They asked if the same might apply to killing and T (the teacher) replied that he would be forced to say "yes". CD (a student) said that while it may seem right *from the point of view of the thief*, he would be taking money from someone who had rightfully earned it, and so it could not possibly be right. T replied with a dilemma: the person who 'rightfully' earns a lot of money and 'rightfully' spends most of it on himself is in effect killing certain people who are dying of starvation somewhere else in the world. CD—it is still different from the stealing case, because he rightfully earned it. T—but perhaps the mere fact that he earned it (forced it out of his consumers) is not a sufficient moral reason for his being morally able to hold on to it. ST (frustratedly)—what *is* a sufficient reason?

EF, CD, KL and others continued to express their uneasiness about the general principle. They felt that it would mean that people would go around stealing, bashing people up ('What about the sadist?'), killing and so on, just because they felt like it. T tried to explain the limits imposed by the dangers of being caught, the need for consistency, the need to get on with other people, and so on, without a great deal of success.

EF wondered how allowing for such radical diversity was compatible with Ginsberg's* claim that the basic moral principles are everywhere fairly much the same. T replied that, on Ginsberg's scheme, the rule about not stealing is a rather specific one, and he does allow for some diversity at this level, as we have already noted."

The reader should note that this part of our work was in the pilot stages and this is reflected in our manner of observation at that time.

*This is a reference to a paper "On the Diversity of Morals" by Morris Ginsberg, from his book *On the Diversity of Morals* (Heinemann, 1956) which was given to the class.

Teaching Format: Springdale

Our work at Springdale Collegiate followed our experience at Campbell. Although our classes had a flexible format, we nevertheless had more initial structure built into the class at Springdale because of the development of curriculum materials*. The classes were 45 minute periods which ran four days a week bi-weekly. In the Fall semester the class was conducted by the major investigators of the project (i.e., Beck and Sullivan). The students sat around a table or grouped with their desks in a circle depending on the classroom available. Our approach to the class varied. During the initial meetings with the students we had a direct discussion of moral theories and principles, using an elementary ethics textbook prepared specifically for use in the high schools (see Beck, 1972). The table of contents which follows will give the reader some indication of the topics discussed:

Part One: What is Morality?

Chapter   1. The Nature of Ethical Inquiry
Chapter   2. Diversity of Moral Codes and the Problem of Objectivity
Chapter   3. The Purpose of Morality
Chapter   4. Justifying Moral Judgments
Chapter   5. The Self and Others
Chapter   6. Favoring an Inner Group
Chapter   7. Justice
Chapter   8. Morality and Compromise

Part Two: Ethics and Psychology

Chapter   9. Elements in Human Moral Psychology
Chapter 10. Different Moral Types
Chapter 11. Theories of Moral Development: Part One
Chapter 12. Theories of Moral Development: Part Two
Chapter 13. Problems in Attaining Moral Maturity

Part Three: Ethics in Today's World

Chapter 14. Politics, Law and Morality
Chapter 15. Business, Economics and Morality
Chapter 16. National, Racial and Cultural Disfunctions

---

*Specifically Beck's textbook on "Ethics" which was designed for use in high schools.

The following is a short excerpt from Chapter 2 which deals with the diversity of moral codes and the problem of objectivity:

> In trying to answer the question 'What is morality?' a consideration of the problem of differences in moral codes is a good starting point. It introduces us immediately to some concrete examples of moral practices and acutely the question 'Is morality objective or is it just a matter of opinion?'

In order to remind ourselves again of the extent of the problem, let us review briefly a number of examples of moral differences, some of them within a particular society, others between societies around the world.

Examples of Diversity in Moral Codes

1. "Criminals" and "respectable citizens" within the same country often have different moral codes, at least in certain respects. For a child brought up in a slum with gangster friends and little chance of getting an education or a job, stealing may be part of his everyday life, something that he values as a way of gaining respect from his friends and obtaining money so that he can pay his rent, buy food and clothing and take out his girl friend. For the respectable citizen it may be essential, for much the same reasons, to remain "respectable" and not allow stealing (at least of an obvious kind) into his system of values and rules.

2. Police and students within the same city often have dif-

ferent values and rules of behavior. Some policemen see the maintenance of public order as a morally valuable end in itself, whereas
some students pursue more personal or more "idealistic" goals at
the expense of public order.

3. In some countries suicide is seen as a crime and a sin; in
others it is considered to be a supreme act of spirituality or
heroism; and in others it is viewed as a mildly unfortunate but interesting phenomenon.

4. In some communities old people are highly respected and
given considerable power; in others they are sent out into the
country by themselves to die; in others they are placed in unpleas-
ant old age homes; and in others they are given the help necessary
to go on living in their own residences or, if they have serious
health problems, are supported in attractive nursing homes.

5. In some communities a man is allowed to have only one
wife; in others it is the custom for a man to have several wives.

6. In some communities it is wrong to eat beef, in others it is
wrong to eat pork, in others it is wrong to eat fish on Fridays, and
in others it is wrong to eat meat of any kind.

7. In some countries, economic equality is considered to be a
more fundamental moral right than economic freedom, whereas in
other countries the opposite view is taken.

These examples give rise to several questions that you may
wish to consider at this stage:

1. Why do people both within our society and around the
world have such different moral beliefs? Is it because people are
different, or because their circumstances are different, or because
morality is just a matter of opinion or taste, or because of something else?

2. Can we criticize the moral beliefs and practices of people
in our own society and in other societies? Can we ever say that
they are wrong in their moral beliefs and practices?

3. Can we be mistaken or wrong in our moral beliefs? Would
it make sense to say "I was mistaken in believing that men who
have three wives are immoral;" or "I was wrong in thinking that I
should never break a promise?" (Beck, 1972).

Some initial discussions were centered on the materials from
part 1 of this book. The use of the text as an introduction was
thought necessary to give all students a semblance of a common
vocabulary and to assist us in overcoming communication problems resulting from a diversity of moral reasoning. When students

tired of text materials they had the option of using a source book*
for the discussion of important social issues or they could bring in
issues of their own. Students always had the option of running the
class along lines they felt most interesting to them. The topics of
discussion ranged over a number of areas. They have included
abortion, capital punishment, drugs, school rules, parents, and
pollution. Some topics would also arise out of current events. The
first part of course was conducted by the two principal investigators of the project and this segment went from September to January. The structured use of the "Ethics" text was completed by
January. The spring term classes were turned over to several of our
colleagues at the Institute who wanted to work with high school
students in this kind of discussion format.

Again, our own objectives for the course would be to stimulate the students to post-conventional thinking. If this occurred,
the students could see that rules and norms have a certain arbi-
trary component about them which make them susceptible to
change when good reasons demand some alteration in conventions.
Realistically, we would be satisfied if each student advanced a
moral stage, even if it were not to the post-conventional level. Our
justification for these objectives is that we see in each higher stage
a more sophisticated form of reasoning which encompasses and in-
tegrates more facets of the problems that contemporary moral
problems present.

Assessment of Moral Reasoning at the Secondary Level

All questionnaires were scored using the latest procedures
available to the authors (see Porter and Taylor, 1972).

Campbell School Results. Apart from the students' personal
assessments we made a more systematic evaluation of the effects
of the class experience by using Kohlberg's Moral Judgment Questionnaire.

Our experimental class completed a written interview on three
separate occasions: at the beginning of the discussion sessions (pre-
test), at the end of the sessions (post-test), and one year after the

---

*We used as a source book "Contemporary Moral Issues". Edited by H.K. Gir-
vetz.

Table 1

A Summary of F Scores Resulting from Analyses of Variance on
Moral Maturity Scores and on Stage Usage Scores
(Taken from Beck, Sullivan and Taylor, 1972)

		Stages			
	MMS	2	3	4	5
Groups (Exp./Control)	.8	—	1.07	1.43	4.58*
Test Time (Pre/Post/Follow Up)	8.32**	1.04	1.78	—	10.84**
Interaction (GroupsXTest Time)	7.58**	2.28	—	1.62	8.10**

*p < .05
**p < .01

end of the sessions (follow-up). Another 17 Grade 11 students from
the same high school but taking an unrelated option served as a
control group and answered the questionnaire at the same time in-
tervals. As a group they were within the same age and IQ range as
the experimental class. A thorough discussion of the results at
Campbell was reported elsewhere (Beck, Sullivan and Taylor,
1972). In this school all but one of the students were predominantly at stages 2, 3 or 4 at all three test times. Since the Moral
Maturity Score (Cf. Porter and Taylor, 1972) provides a quantita-
tive score of moral reasoning level we used it as a basis for our
first evaluation of class sessions. The results of an analysis of
variance on these scores are shown in Table 1. Both the Test Time

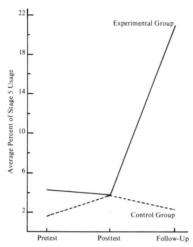

Figure 6. Mean percentage of stage 5 usage for each
group at each test time. (Beck, Sullivan
and Taylor, 1972).

factor and the interaction of Groups and Test time were significant
at the .01 level. A further analysis of the simple main effects (ne-
cessitated by the significant interaction) indicated that the two
groups differed significantly at the Follow-Up testing though not
at the Pre and Post Tests, and that significant changes in the
MMS scores over the three test times occurred only for the Experimental group. A Neuman-Keuls comparison of the different mean
MMS's confirmed these findings and further indicated that the
Test Time effect for the Experimental group was due to the large
increase in MMS at the Follow-Up.

The overall MMS, thus, suggested some effect of the classroom experiences on moral reasoning one year after the end of
the classes (though not immediately after). Since the MMS is a
composite of usage of the different stages, we reexamined the data
to see whether the changes in MMS were due to changes in the
amount of some stages being used over others.

For our students the amount of stage 1 and stage 6 thinking
was negligible and was ignored. Analyses of variance, similar to
the one used on the MMS's, were done on the percentage usage

scores for stages 2, 3, 4 and 5 and are summarized in Table 1. The obtained differences in percentage usage of stages 2, 3, and 4 for the two groups and at the three test times would appear to be due to chance. For stage 5, however, both the main factors and their interaction were significant. Though the interaction took a slightly different form from that with the MMS's, the results were very similar and thus are diagrammed in Figure 6. Again a further analysis of the main effects showed that the two groups differed in stage 5 usage at the Follow-Up (though not at the Pre and Post Tests) and that the changes over Test Time occurred only for the Experimental Group. The Newman-Keuls comparison of mean percentage scores confirmed this and indicated again that these changes for the Experimental group were due to a large increase in stage 5 usage at the Follow-Up.

To summarize, it would seem that the increase in moral reasoning level at the Follow-Up for the Experimental Group was the result of an increase in stage 5 thinking. In fact a simple head count of students who had stage 5 thinking at all showed that while only 4 students used stage 5 at the Pre Test (2 Experimental, 2 control), two-thirds of the students in the Experimental class used some stage 5 thinking at the Follow-Up as compared to about one-tenth of the Control group. (The Post Test counts differed little from those of the Pre Test.)

Springdale Collegiate Results. This experimental class was given the Moral Judgment Interview on three separate occasions. Once at the beginning of the discussion sessions (pretest), at the end of the course (posttest), and one year after the end of the course (follow-up). A control group was given a pretest but for various reasons beyond our control we were unable to give them the posttest or follow-up assessments. It was therefore, impossible to make the comparisons that we made in the Campbell study. We nevertheless plotted a profile in major stage usage in the Experimental group to see if there would be a comparable phenomenon occurring as in the Campbell study (i.e.; a dramatic increase in stage 5 reasoning in our class). As can be seen in Figure 7 and from Table 2, there was no significant increase in stage 5 reasoning, although there is a trend in that direction in the follow-up assessment. Table 2 shows Moral Maturity Scores and stage usage

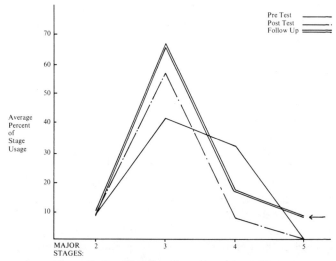

Figure 7. Profile of major stage usage on pre-, post-, and follow-up-tests for experimental subjects.

Table 2

Analysis of Variance of
Moral Maturity Scores (MMS) and Stage Usage Scores over
Pre- Post- and Follow-Up-Tests
Experimental Subjects

Summary of F Scores

	F Ratio
MMS	.2960
Stage 2	.3178
Stage 3	3.1767**
Stage 4	1.0667
Stage 5	.4763

**Sig. 05   Cf. Winer, 1962, p. 112ff.

scores over Pre-, Post-, and Follow-Up tests. Analysis of variance indicated that there was significantly more stage 3 thinking when compared to other stage usage (i.e.; stages 2, 4 and 5). Note, too, from a developmental perspective, there is no stage 1 or stage 6 thinking in this adolescent group.

The predominance of stage 3 thinking in our Springdale students is quite consistent with the normative data that we have gathered for our Canadian population in Figure 3 (see p. 17). It is clear from the populations we have assessed that the modal stage response for adolescents between the ages of 15 and 18 years is stage 3. This does not explain why there is a discrepancy between our Springdale and Campbell students. Developmentally, we had hoped that our course would encourage post-conventional moral reasoning and we had reason to believe that it would from our findings at Campbell High School. In spite of the post-conventional content of the "Ethics" text used, our Springdale students did not show an expected significant increase in stage 5 reasoning at the end of the course (post-test) or a year later (follow-up).*

The discrepancy between the Springdale and Campbell studies made us reflect on the possible way that the two courses differed. Several possible differences came to mind. First, the teaching format changed when we worked with the Springdale students. We used a structured textbook in Springdale that was not used in Campbell. Although the content was post-conventional in orientation, it nevertheless reflected the initial interests of the teachers and not the students. This may have put the students in a conventional set to accept our ideas as a source of expert authority. One cannot guarantee that the students will treat post-conventional content in a post-conventional manner. The fact that the text was considered required by the instructors for at least some parts of the course could have encouraged an attitude of treating us as unquestioned authorities since one of the instructors was the writer of the textbook. Second, the Springdale class differed from Campbell in the number of instructors who taught the class. In Campbell, only one instructor taught the class for a semester. At Springdale the

---

*Note however in Figure 7 that there is an increase in stage 5 thinking but this trend is not statistically significant as in the Campbell study.

classes were led by five different instructors. The first semester classes were with the two major directors of the project (Beck and Sullivan) who worked jointly with the students and the second semester classes were conducted by three other OISE colleagues who conducted the class individually. The presence of so many different instructors may have caused the course to become disorganized because of so many different points of view. Probably the most beneficial arrangement was at the Campbell school where there was a sustained post-conventional orientation given by one teacher. Third, we felt a difference in the school atmospheres could have also been a factor for the discrepancy in the results between the two schools. Even from the Campbell study we would have to conclude that our course by itself did not produce the significant increase in stage 5 reasoning since there was no significant difference between the experimental and control group at the end of the course (i.e.; post-test). The change occurred one year later (i.e.; follow-up) in an interim in which no course in ethics was offered. Our own feeling was that our course interacted with other significant factors in the school atmosphere to produce the increase in stage 5 reasoning. In other words our ethics course was a catalyst for change, when combined with other factors. Our own subjective evaluation of the two secondary schools that we have worked in is that they are different in atmosphere. We felt that Campbell was more open and democratic in structure when compared with Springdale. There was also a difference between the cooperating teachers in the two schools that we feel may have been significant. Our cooperating teacher at Campbell was much more permissive with us and with his class. He did not participate in class discussion and was completely unobtrusive when we were running the classes. He picked up on points in his classes which were raised in the classes we ran. The cooperating teacher at Springdale was quite different. In general he participated in class discussions and was very authoritarian in his demeanor. He interrupted students and caused considerable tensions as far as we were concerned. We finally made an arrangement whereby he would not be present in the classes we conducted. In contrast to the follow-up work of the Campbell teacher, we felt that the Springdale teacher conducted classes in a manner alien to our objectives in the moral education course. The more *authoritarian* atmosphere of Springdale appeared to be exemplified in our cooperating teacher.

Our experience working in two high schools made us aware of the "hidden curriculum" discussed by critics of the school. We became much more sensitive to how the structure of the school can implicitly encourage a certain kind of morality and to be more specific, an authoritarian conventional one. Many of the efforts of individual teachers to help students toward a post-conventional (stage 5 or 6) level of moral development are frustrated by a school atmosphere and organization which constantly emphasizes lower stage values and principles. Or, to put the point more positively, a school atmosphere and organization which exhibits post-conventional features can greatly facilitate the development of students towards the higher moral stages. Unfortunately, most school systems are run on broadly authoritarian lines, and a relationship of mutual trust, respect and co-operation between student and teacher is extremely difficult to cultivate in such an environment.

There are many things which teachers can do to create the appropriate environment in the classroom. To begin with, they can learn to have intellectual humility and a willingness to admit ignorance, acknowledge a mistake, or modify views in the face of sound counterarguments by students. The teacher should not pose as an intellectual genius or as an infallible source of knowledge. There are considerable pressures upon him from parents, the public, and even the students to maintain such a posture, but he must resist these forces. In particular, teachers must learn to give full acknowledgement of, and make constant use of, the expertise of students. Only in this way can a spirit of cooperative search for knowledge and wisdom be developed in the classroom.

In general, the teacher should show respect for the student as a person. This is easily said and repeated; but we often overlook the enormous backlog of authoritarianism toward younger people which exists in society. Permissiveness is not what is needed; that is not respect: we are only "permissive" to inferiors. The teacher must treat students as other *people*, who have a diversity of abilities and desires (just as he has), and with whom he happens to be engaged in certain semipersonal cooperative activities. He has been given a degree of authority over them, that is true; but he should exercise that authority only insofar as a sizable majority are convinced that it is necessary for the cooperative activities in which they are engaged. He is a resource person, chairman, leader; but he should exercise these roles only insofar as it is deemed useful by the group. If most of the students in a class feel at a particular point that such a role is not needed, or that someone could fill it better, that settles the matter. All those people are unlikely to be wrong although they could be.

There are many little things which can help. Seating arrangements can be changed. First names can be used. Students can speak without raising their hands. Students can speak directly to each other in group discussions rather than through the teacher. These things are not particularly important in themselves, and their appropriateness may vary with the size and age level of the group. However, they may serve as significant symbols of an underlying relationship of mutual respect.

But while these arrangements and relationships are being established in the classroom, the school as a whole may be militating against the objectives of the particular teacher. There is a great deal of research to be carried out in the area of non-authoritarian school organization and its effects upon moral development. Some experiments have been performed and there are various books and articles on free schools, open-plan schools, and non-authoritarian schools in general. It is difficult to draw conclusions from these experiments. Many of the free schools have been either too small, or too short-lived, or too unusual in some other way to enable us to make predictions about what might happen in a large school in a total system. Open-plan schools have been tried fairly extensively over a long period in some areas, but where they have succeeded it is difficult to tell why, and there have been many failures. Furthermore, it is questionable whether open-plan schools, working within a basically authoritarian system, can really be non-authoritarian. Sometimes, perhaps, they become even more authoritarian than usual, because of the difficulties of maintaining conventional "order" in an open-plan situation. This highlights the basic problem of bringing about institutional changes favorable to moral development in the schools: it is difficult to change the classroom without a change in the structural arrangements and authority channels of the school itself.

We are also struck by the possibility of the teachers' moral level influencing the classroom discussion. Although it would be unfair to belabor our point about the Springdale experience, we believe that it is indicative of a more pervasive phenomenon in the teaching profession. There is usually a selective process in education and ordinarily, teachers who are successful in professional educational circles have conventional moral values. This is not necessarily an indictment of the teaching profession since there are many good reasons which give support to conventional morality. The school is an agent of socialization and part of its mandate is to help parents and society, in general, in the inculcation of conventional moral norms. No one would argue that contemporary schooling is failing in its attempt at this mandate. The only problem is that much of conventional morality does not match up with the problems presented to the student in contemporary society. In school he is learning conventional morals that appear archaic to his own life space. We do not wish to argue that everything new under the "moral sun" has an aura of sanctity about it, but it is imperative with our rapidly changing value systems to examine both old and new values alike. The problem with most teacher training institutions is that they are the fortress of most conventional norms. The teacher who finishes training is well aware of the "tried and true" conventions that have kept the school going for years. These conventions are known as the collective wisdom which all new teachers need in order to get by and succeed in their task. The final outcome of this whole process, which is subsequently supported by the very structure of the school itself, is a predominance of teachers who remain for the most part in the conventional stages (stages 3 and 4) of morality. The emphasis on "law and order" in the school is important but as we shall see later it inhibits some aspects of the educational process.

Specific to our discussion is the teacher's level or stage of moral development in the classroom where moral and ethical issues are being discussed. Our own conviction is that it is important to have teachers at a post-conventional level of morality, so as to stimulate higher levels of moral reasoning in students. This does not necessarily make the teacher a moral rebel or a danger to school order. In most instances post-conventional moral arguments recognize the need for conventions but they base the merits of the conventions on sound reasoning rather than on some unquestioned authority source. There are also discussions on contemporary social issues which will take students and the teacher into areas where there are no clear authoritative sources. The teacher must indicate to the student his own fallibility on matters such as these, if and when they arise in a classroom discussion. It would seem difficult for stage 4 conventional "law and order" teachers to put themselves in this kind of a role because there will be a latent fear that if the teacher does not have all the answers, his classroom authority will be relinquished. Since the structure of the class usually leaves the teacher in a controlling position, he is typically the initial modulator of the level of the classroom discussion. If the teacher's emphasis is on the maintenance of "law and order" and "authority," the discussion is not likely to venture into levels where authority is questioned on rational grounds.

V
Teacher Education

Our reflections from the previous chapter dramatized the importance of teacher education where values in education are concerned. It is in the area of teacher training, however, that we feel least confident in making policy judgments. Because of limitations on the charter of the Ontario Institute for Studies in Education there is no formal teacher training carried out at the Institute. Therefore our interest in teacher training could be only pursued through indirect means. One of the areas of indirect means has been through the development of workshops in value education for teachers and administrative personnel. Throughout the first four years of the Moral Education Project various groups have requested one day workshop meetings on the broad implications of our work. At first we felt that such requests should be denied on the grounds that one day sessions are not sufficient except for a superficial examination of issues. On the other hand, the genuine concern of parents, administrators, university students, local boards merited an attempt to provide information and hopefully impetus to these groups to undertake a long range study of moral education. From the start the second consideration has outweighed the first.

Initially, the decision to offer short sessions for the many groups who requested assistance was a pragmatic one. The Ontario Institute for Studies in Education emphasizes dissemination as much as research. Workshops are a simple, if not necessarily effective way, of fulfilling this task of reporting on work in progress. However as the moral education project developed from a classroom research venture to one of teacher-consultant training the workshop events became an opportunity for identifying current concerns of practitioners and testing approaches for both responding and revising these concerns.

Two basic formats for workshops are available. The first is a lecture approach: outlining in general terms current philosophic, psychological and educational theories for moral education. In this method the workshop leader anticipates questions and concerns. He can organize material efficiently and in two or three hours provide a framework of information for participants. A second format incorporates learning principles fundamental to cognitive moral development in what we call an "episode approach." Participants are immediately confronted with a situation involving a range of moral/value issues. They discuss a particular episode: identify issues, argue positions, hear a variety of points of view.

Our experiences with short-term workshops has led us to view them in somewhat problematic terms. We are skeptical of their impact in the area of teacher training and at best, the outcomes of such sessions leave the participants with a) some knowledge of new developments in the field of moral education, b) an awareness of the pervasiveness of value issues in the content and style of all school programs and c) a commitment on the part of a small number of participants to follow-up study and experimentation in moral education programs in their own specialty. It is this type of extended interest and motivation which encouraged us to attempt a course at the Ontario Institute labelled "Practicum in Value Education." The description of the course indicated that it would be geared to teachers involved in the area of moral education and related areas (e.g., Social Studies, Humanities, Religious Education, etc.). In addition to the applied bent for teachers, the course was also designed to give practical in-school experience for full-time M.A. and Ph.D. students who are enrolled in the Departments of Applied Psychology and History and Philosophy. The outcome of our experience with this practicum is the content of this chapter.

Objectives of the Practicum

Seven students were enrolled in the practicum from January through April 1973 (i.e., four teachers and three full time graduate students). All of the course members had at least one course previously in the area of moral theory. It was stressed to all members that the practicum was experimental in nature and thus changes in procedure could be expected as the occasion demanded. Our objectives for the teachers involved were as follows:

(1) To acquaint them with pertinent contemporary literature in moral development. Specifically, this involved several readings from our edited volume on moral education (i.e., Beck, Crittenden and Sullivan, 1971).

(2) To introduce them to the materials that we prepared while teaching in the High Schools. Specifically, they were given copies of Beck's (1972) book on "Ethics" for high school students. It was their option to use this material in their teaching if they deemed it appropriate.

(3) To provide a format for discussion around issues and problems in moral education and more specifically issues and problems that were raised by the practicum. To this end, four major meetings of all participants in the course were scheduled from the beginning to the end of the practicum.

(4) To have feedback from an observer who would be working with them in some of their scheduled classes. Specifically the observer was one of the full time graduate students who was enrolled in the practicum.

Our objectives for the full time graduate students involved were as follows:

(1) To give them some experience in the classroom related to topics in the moral sphere. Each of the three graduate students was paired with one of the teachers involved.

(2) To help them to develop observation skills which might be pertinent to teacher training in this area. These students were observers in an observer-teacher team relationship.

(3) To develop skills in the assessment of moral reasoning. All three graduate students were given a three day workshop where they learned to score Kohlberg's moral judgment protocols. The

workshop enabled students to administer and score the moral judgment protocols of the students in the classes that they were observ-
ing.

(4) To help them form a working relationship with teachers in
a school setting. Our four meetings were designed to facilitate
feedback between the observers and teachers.

The practicum teachers taught in four different high schools
and a short description of three of these school experiences is appropriate here*.

SCHOOL A

The Teacher-Observer Pair

Our teacher in school A was a male Vice-Principal of a suburban high school. He was very interested in the area of Ethics and
saw the practicum as a way to pursue his interests. He did not normally hold classes and his participation in the practicum was
through an arrangement with one of the "World Religion" teachers in his school. He took two classes a week of the "World Religion" course for discussion of ethical and moral issues. His role in
the school was primarily administrative with the exception of this
course.

All our observers were female. The observer in school A was
one of the moderators of the Ministry preparation course for the
Presbyterian church. She had been involved in religious education
for many years and was enrolled as a full time Ph.D. candidate in
the "Interdisciplinary" program at the Institute. Her program included the disciplines of Adult Education, Applied Psychology and
History and Philosophy. She had taken several courses related to
the area of moral education at the Institute and saw the practicum
as a means of concretizing her interests in this area.

Description of the School and Students

School A is located in a fairly affluent suburb of Toronto and

---

*One of our teachers enrolled late in the course and we were unable to send an ob-
server to his school. We therefore omit the description of his work here.

the students were above average in intelligence test scores. The class that participated in the experimental moral education program was a senior level (grades 11 and 12) group which was also involved in experimental work in a World Religions course. This World Religions course was taught during the whole school year by a teacher not affiliated with the practicum. From mid-January to mid-May 1973 approximately two of the five class periods per week were devoted to moral education discussions taught by Teacher A. Each class period was forty minutes in length.

Twenty students took part in this phase of the course and the class consisted of five boys and fifteen girls. Their ages ranged from 15 to 18 years. Their intelligence quotients were above average. They were given the Kohlberg Moral Judgment Questionnaire by the classroom observer over three class sessions. At the beginning of the course there was a dominance of stage 3 (i.e., Good-Boy-Nice-Girl) with some stage 2 and stage 4 thinking. Only one student gave evidence of post-conventional stage 5 reasoning.

Description of Course Content

This teacher used selections from Beck's (1972) textbook on "Ethics" as a basis for discussion in class. Six topics were covered throughout the course: (1) Justice (2) Our Relationship with Poor and Unemployed (3) Our Relationship with the Sick and the Question of Euthanasia (4) Justifying Moral Judgments (5) The Self and Others and (6) Compromise and Morality. All of these topics had corresponding reading material from the "Ethics" text.

Critical Reflections of Teacher A*

Teacher A felt he had varying success with the class depending on the topic area being discussed. Of particular interest are some of his comments on some of the topic areas that he covered. On the topic of *Justice*:

Naturally the concept of Justice was a most interesting topic for these students. Perhaps because of their socio-economic background, perhaps because of the influence of violence in

*The authors are grateful to the teachers and observers who submitted written reports of their work and from whom we freely quote.

today's society, perhaps because of man's innate nature to be somewhat selfish, this teacher cannot be certain of which of these, it was however unanimously agreed upon that *Justice did not exist*. Not a student was pursuing Justice as an ultimate goal and not a student believed that Justice existed as such. People were puppets who were basically afraid to give other people *what they deserve*.

On the topic of *Our Relationship with the Poor and Unemployed*:

It was a shock to this teacher to see the attitude of these students toward the poor and the unemployed. Not only did they not feel any responsibility to them, they almost felt repulsed at the idea of talking about it. Many felt that we were spoiling the poor by having such an easy welfare system, others felt that employment was available fairly easily for those who wished to work, most of them agreed that our present economic system was simply a confirmation of their belief that Justice did not exist. 'What ever happened to Justice for the rich?', was a phrase tossed out on a number of occasions, in classroom discussions.

On the topic of *Our Relationship with the Sick and the Question of Euthanasia*:

It was equally amazing to see the attitude of these students towards the ill and oppressed. Many felt that everyone had a contribution to make to society but when that contribution was completed society was there to be enjoyed. If, on the other hand, you were becoming a burden on the society, be that society as a whole, or your immediate society, namely, your family, then, it was perfectly morally correct to quietly and painlessly send you to a better world. The impression that this teacher really received was that this world was for the young and strong and for those people able to make a contribution and willing to make this world a better place. Justice was not being served by asking people to give up what they had so that other people, presumably contributing nothing, could be looked after.

It seems obvious from the reflections of Teacher A that these topics pulled stage 2 thinking (i.e., naive instrumental hedonism) which we knew was present in these students' thinking because of its presence on their moral judgment protocols. A further amplification of this can be seen in this teacher's observations on the unit from Beck's "Ethics" text called the *Self and Others*:

A number of examples were presented here by the teacher, starting from the self-situation and then, expanding it to include eventually an Inner Group. The idea of *'Doing your own thing'*, was discussed thoroughly and the students found that the whole *concept* could not be defined without involving other people. Just the same, what soon became quite clear to both students and teacher, was that the Self in relationship with others, even those in the inner group, will almost always act in a way beneficial to him. The idea of sacrificing one's self for the benefit of an inner group is something of the past and certainly not predominant among young people today. Peer pressure is perhaps the strongest influence that students receive and this was extremely well demonstrated in discussions about Shoplifting or Cheating on tests or the like. It was most interesting to discover for example, that most students would react the following way, if they saw a friend 'shoplifting' especially if that friend happened to be a member of their inner group. They would:

-ignore it or walk up behind the student and cough so that he would know that he had been seen,

-have a talk with the student later and try to persuade him to return the merchandise; or,

-never report him to the manager of the store.

If however, the person doing the shoplifting was not a friend or an acquaintance, in most cases, the students felt they would report him to the store manager because it was their *moral obligation to do so* and that's how young people get a bad name, and so forth. The students saw absolutely nothing wrong with this double standard. Students felt completely justified in not reporting a friend because . . . a friend knows what your needs are. The store has a lot of material and goods so they will not miss a little but . . . but your friend might have to go to jail for it—or have a record of some type. Nothing would sway the students' point of view on this matter as they felt totally justified in their thoughts.

A final note from this teacher on the unit labelled *Compromise* reiterates the themes we have already noted and also brings up a point of discretion as to the appropriateness of certain topics for high school students:

> For the most part the discussions on *compromise* were a disaster. Though not as difficult as originally anticipated, they proved to be a disaster because I did not research the class enough beforehand. Students today are willing to compromise in most situations, as long as they or their inner group are not going to get too hurt by decisions reached.

> This teacher *attacked* the subject of *abortion*. To be absolutely fair, I arranged for local doctors to visit the class and present different points of views. Religion never entered the picture; we dealt with the subject from a moral viewpoint. One week a doctor spoke in favor of abortion on demand and answered a number of questions. The following week, a second doctor spoke against abortion on demand and also answered several questions. Following that, we had a number of classes, with several staff members of the school attending, and we held many lively discussions. Morally speaking, students are not in favor of abortion on demand (for the most part) but they also feel that it should be easily available for those who wish it.

> Morally, it is against their principles but they are willing to sacrifice these principles (or to compromise) for others' sake. When the question inevitably came up as to whether they would be willing to undergo an abortion, it was a different story. While students are opposed to abortion in theory, many felt they would have an abortion if need be . . . and most agreed that it would be for selfish reasons . . . such as, why ruin my life?, why go through the trouble?, etc., etc. It would not be an easy decision but most felt they would sacrifice their principles and accept the compromise.

> However, it should be pointed out here that topics of this nature should be cautioned against, in future years. It is near-impossible to maintain a satisfactory level of discussion and attempt to bring in Values, in a topic of this type. Conclusions are inevitably reached and students are just forced to take too hard a look at themselves. After all, they are a captive audience and do not have the choice of being there or leaving.

While this topic may be excellent, it is also *very dangerous*. In this class, the sister of one of the students had just undergone an abortion. Needless to say, the situation at home was not the best there is and the teacher was not aware of it until later. The discussion of Values, attached to the subject, was certainly not appropriate for that student. I can't help but feel that perhaps more damage was done . . . for that student . . . by bringing up the topic in the first place. In future years, perhaps it should be suggested that topics such as Abortion be avoided. During the students' high school years, it is still a very tender and impressionable topic.

Naturally, this topic was dropped rather quickly thereafter but we continued to discuss the concept of Compromise by bringing in a number of moral dilemmas where something or someone had to be sacrificed in favor of another. Students responded well in these areas, and it was interesting to see their reasoning and how, for many, the reasons were so different than at the beginning of the course on Value Education, in early January. Again and still, the peer pressure and the inner group influence is very much in evidence here.

Teacher A brought this course to a conclusion by using text material from Beck on the topic of "Ethics and Psychology". He felt that much of this material duplicated a course in psychology that was offered in that school. When the students were introduced to different types of moral thinking, as illustrated in Kohlberg's theory, they started classifying each other. At this point students generated their own moral dilemmas and tried to analyze how and why they would choose a certain course of action. The teacher felt that for him, this was the most satisfying part of the course since he felt the tenor of the discussions indicated some development when compared with the beginning of the course. The course concluded with a post-test on Kohlberg's moral reasoning dilemmas, the teacher indicating that he was interested in seeing if their answers and reasons would be different than what they had written originally at the beginning of the course. The students appeared to look forward to the task.

Teacher A felt that the text material from Beck's Ethics textbook was too advanced for this class. Specifically, he found that the vocabulary was too advanced for high school students. It was his opinion that the book assumed too much of the students on definitions pertaining to ethical concepts.

Critical Reflections of Observer A

Observer A saw the teacher in class once a week. She indicated from her observation that Teacher A had a relaxed classroom manner and the students liked him more as they came to know him better. This is important insofar as this was not the teacher's regular class and he was also the Vice-Principal of the school. Rapport and trust became obvious when students related school pranks which were contrary to school regulations.

The observer took a different view as to why Beck's "Ethics" text was not as successful as it could have been for the course.

> As a means of assessing the usefulness of Clive Beck's "Ethics" as a high school text, this class experiment was inadequate. Only part of the material was used and that in a rather haphazard manner. The book itself was not used at all. Mimeographed copies of sections of the manuscript were handed out to students chapter by chapter. I believe that, for high school youth, a mimeographed manuscript appears less interesting and impressive than a printed book. In addition, interested students had no opportunity to read ahead and see the relationship of chapter to chapter.

The observer felt that a text was important in a course of this nature. She felt that the text was not given a fair chance and noted that when it was dropped discussions took place without benefit of factual research. This observer felt that because of this lack of proper research the discussions, in many instances, appeared superficial and uninformed. This tendency to superficial treatment of topics raised the question in the observer's mind as to what the reaction the students were actually having to the course:

> They seemed happy enough to spend the class time either discussing or listening to a discussion of a topic. They enjoyed exchanging ideas with the teacher or listening to such an exchange. . . . However, with little to read (except for occasional chapters of Beck's book early in the term), with no assignments for study or research, and with no examination or tests (other than the Kohlberg dilemmas for which they knew

they would not be graded) one wonders whether they considered the unit a 'mickey mouse' course that demanded little of them.

The structure of the discussions was consistent from observer A's point of view. In all the class sessions that she observed at this school, with the exception of the one in which students did individual work on duplicated copies of a moral dilemma, the one teaching method used by teacher A would be labelled teacher-centered discussion. Practically all discussions originated with and was directed toward him; only occasionally did students speak directly to each other in general discussion.

This teacher-centered format has implications for moral education when one considers the hidden curriculum in the school as regards authority maintainence. As this observer noted:

. . . . During discussions Mr. (Teacher A) established an easy relationship with the students. There was freedom for them to express ideas and viewpoints. Indeed, even though he was a vice-principal, they told, in relation to a point they were making in discussion, that some of them had entered the school by a window they knew was not locked during the preceeding holiday week-end to get some materials (their own) that they wanted to work on. Such freedom seemed indicative of a good relationship which they had with the school staff. . . .

Mr. (Teacher A) did have considerable skill in leading discussion. He formulated good questions to stimulate thinking. He was able to make statements with 'tongue in cheek' to obtain student reaction. He was sensitive to student feelings.

However he made no attempt to involve students in contributing to the initiation of discussion through panels, debates, role play, etc. Nor did he attempt to aid the more reticent students to contribute by using triads, buzz groups or other small group techniques.

As a result the number of students contributing to discussion in any one class period was usually limited to ten or eleven at the most and it was usually the same ten or eleven who spoke at all class sessions. Indeed discussion tended to be dominated throughout by the teacher and a maximum of 5 or 6 students. . . . Many of the more silent members appeared to be interested in the discussions, though at times some looked bored and some spent part of the time reading. While a teacher must respect the wishes of a student to be silent at times, he also has responsibility for trying to involve each student in the learning process and for endeavoring to discover what actual learning each student is accomplishing.

Experience in this classroom however raises questions related to the possibility of attempts at indoctrination in values education classes. One wants to raise such questions as: 'Whose values will be taught?' 'Does the teacher express his own point of view?' In a sense the class represents a captive audience. Care needs to be taken against indoctrination. Yet if the teacher has a good relationship with the students, he may, it seems, suggest his point of view as one possible solution, accept other viewpoints presented by the students, and give the students freedom to make their own choices and decisions.

The observer felt that this teacher had accomplished this type of atmosphere.

Finally, observer A was fortunate in pre-testing and post-testing the students of this class on Kohlberg's moral judgment scale. No statistical analysis was carried out so the following observations are just for interest. Perusal of the protocols indicated that seven students showed no change in stage orientation from pre-test to post-test, ten students appeared to be in transitional stages indicating small advances, one student advanced a complete stage, one appeared to have regressed slightly.

Summary Evaluation of the Practicum Experience

Both the teacher and observer seemed to be satisfied with their practicum experience. The teacher felt that the sounding of the students indicated a favorable response to the ethics section of the "World Religions" course of which it was a part. In the last class he conducted a survey to see how the students felt about the course. He maintained that the feedback was positive but all students felt that the course should be longer, perhaps a full year. They also indicated how important it was that a teacher in a course be flexible and willing to allow students to go off on tangents. They had a strong taste against a lecture type format for this type of class.

Both the teacher and the observer felt that the practicum had raised many questions in their mind as to just how and where moral education was to fit into the school curriculum. The observer in school A had several recommendations for consideration as a result of her experience. First, she thought that the policy of having a Moral Education Practicum should be continued for another year to permit additional classroom experimentation. Second, that teachers in their own classrooms be observed by full time OISE students acting as observers and, that in all future practicums of this nature, all participants (observers and teachers) participate in the workshop on Kohlberg's stages. In this practicum only the observers participated in the practicum. Third, that some additional help be given to the observers concerning what to observe, how to record observations, etc. (e.g., perhaps a mimeographed sheet of suggestions). Fourth, that this program of observation be planned so that, in order to see some continuity in a sequence of lessons, an observer could observe *all* classes in a specific unit of the moral education program and then only occasional classes. Fifth, that regular consultations between teacher and observer be required to provide for (a) informing the observer about objectives, unit and lesson plans, and related information, and (b) providing a feedback from observer to teacher. Sixth, that a post-course reaction form be provided so that the observer and teacher can secure course reactions from the high school students participating in the experiment. Seventh, that provision be made for observers to pay single visits to at least one or preferably two other classrooms involved in the project. Eighth, that teachers be given some suggestions regarding a variety of teaching techniques to encourage student involvement in moral education classes. Finally, that teachers be encouraged to give some individual and class assignments so that students may be encouraged to put some serious effort into the work of the course.

SCHOOL B

The Teacher-Observer Pair

Teacher B was a male history teacher. He was enrolled part time at OISE at the Master's level. He had some elementary background in moral philosophy and was interested in the practicum in order to improve his teaching of history.

Observer B was a female who was a full time Master's candidate in the Department of Applied Psychology. She had an undergraduate degree in Psychology and since she was a newly enrolled student in graduate school she had had no advanced courses in ethics or moral philosophy. Her interest in the practicum was to give an applied bent to her course work which was heavily oriented in psychological theory and research.

Description of School and Students

School B was located in a suburb of Toronto and the students were predominately from a middle-class background and of average intelligence. It was an eleventh grade class in the subject of History.

Observer B assessed these students on Kohlberg's moral judgment scale at the start of the course but did not have an opportunity to post-test them at the completion of the course. The majority of these students were at the conventional level of moral judgment (i.e., stage 3 and 4), 14 out of 25 students were dominant stage 3 in their thinking. Five students had minor stage 4 and four had minor stage 2 as their sub-stage. As in school A, students in school B showed predominantly stage 3 thinking on Kohlberg's moral judgment questionnaire. Only three students in school B displayed post-conventional thinking (i.e., stage 5) but even here it could not be considered enough to be counted as even a minor stage.

Description of Course Content

Teacher B's purpose in using materials with ethical impact in his History course was in order to personalize his History classes. Concurrent with the use of moral education materials for a deepening of historical understanding, this teacher also hoped that the study of history would not only help students clarify their substantive values but provide experience in reasoning out ethical dilemmas. The course was entitled "Ideas Which Shaped the World". The general goals for students involved encouragement of an understanding of various concepts of government and freedom. This demanded that students become familiarized with, and examine such notions as humanism, individualism, skepticism, secularism and rationalism. Various types of government were examined and the students were introduced to several philosophers or key figures in the development of social order. The philosophies of such men as Hitler, Eric Hoffer, Locke, Rousseau, Machiavelli, Hobbes, etc. were discussed. The teacher states his content objectives for the course as follows:

. . . . (a) to suggest that the historical account is open to question, (b) to show that certain ideas have changed as society has changed, (the concept of the good man, for example, in Medieval, Renaissance, and Industrial periods in Europe), (c) to show that certain assumptions, values, and philosophies are taken for granted by our society, (d) to show the development of modern Western society as the development of certain ideas through time (e.g., humanism, rationalism, capitalism). . . . The course was an introduction to senior history, which at School B makes great use of the seminar and required individual research and essay writing. Moreover, given content objective (a), skill objectives of the type that follow are extremely important. They are: (a) to explain scientific method as it pertains to history and provide practice in its use, (b) to explain and provide practice in library procedure, (c) to explain and provide practice in the construction of reasoned argument based on documented evidence, (d) to provide practice in identifying and attacking arguments presented by others.

So far as values were concerned the course was designed: (a) to develop within the student attitudes and values conducive to systematic learning, (b) to develop an enjoyment of the study of history, (c) to develop an enjoyment of mental challenge, (d) to show students that they can achieve if they persist.

Secondarily, on a skills level, he hoped that students would gain some experience in moral reasoning and, on a values level, that they would become more aware of the processes and criteria

Table 3

Integration of Moral Education and Historical Material to Form
Coherent Units

Unit Title

The Renaissance explained as a change in what men valued.

General Questions to be Examined

1. What is a value?
2. Does what a person values affect what a person does?
3. How can one find out what another values?
4. What did St. Thomas Aquinas, A Medieval Man, value?
5. What did Leonardo DaVinci value?
6. How do Medieval and Renaissance values seem to differ?

Unit Title

Ideas and Their Suppression.

General Questions to be Examined

1. If someone is convinced that he knows the truth
   a) is he morally obliged to proselytize
   b) can the idea be orally suppressed by others?
2. What new ideas were presented by Copernicus and Galileo?
3. Why did the Church attempt to suppress them?
4. What was the result of the widespread adoption among learned men of the Copernician system?

Unit Title

Trust.

General Questions

1. What is trust?
2. Under what circumstances should it be exercised?
3. What did Christ, Machiavelli and Hitler have to say about trust?
4. What assumptions did each hold about man?

Integration of Moral Education and Historical Material to Form
Coherent Units

Materials beyond the historical took three forms. Use was made of some
parts of Beck's text despite its advanced reading level. Dilemmas were
utilized, some borrowed, some modified and some manufactured. Some
use was made of games.

In the unit on trust we played a game designed to prove that most class
members simply did not trust other class members. We then brainstormed
the whole ideas of trust and trusting.

by which moral judgments are made, and might clarify their substantive values to some degree. In organizing the course he tried to
integrate moral education and historical material to form coherent
units. There follow three examples taken from the course outline
(see Table 3).

It is clear from the above that teacher B subordinated moral
education into the more inclusive goals of a history course.

Critical Reflections of Teacher B

Teacher B's perception of his role in the class can be seen in
the following reflection:

Classes were run in a very informal style. Students knew that
requirements were high, and that I expected effort and improvement from them. On the other hand, to get this, I used
positive reinforcement as much as possible. I encouraged
rather than chided. I praised any improvement and attempted
to provide rapid feedback by marking and returning papers
quickly.

Since it was important for the success of the course that students felt free to approach me for aid I disciplined through
cajolery and attempted to maintain a very relaxed atmosphere
in class. The result was a fairly honest sharing of experiences
by a proportion of the group.

In methodology I prefer a Fentonian approach. I like to challenge the group and then let the students work out the problem as independently as possible. My role takes three forms. I offer input both in content and in method. I act as devil's advocate occasionally. I moderate discussion among students.

The course was successful enough to encourage further effort. At semester's end I assigned an evaluation which in part asked students to identify major themes within the course. An encouraging number were able to state the ideas expressed in the content objectives listed earlier. This in itself is not spectacular but within their evaluations several students mentioned as a strength of the course that it related history to the present well and so made the subject interesting. They specifically mentioned discussions we had had on ethical problems and the way these had been used to make history more immediate and real. I am left attempting to identify problem areas within the course so that modifications may be made. Firstly, enough students mentioned suffering from initial confusion to reinforce my own feeling that attempting to build two sets of cumulative concepts simultaneously may be beyond reasonable expectations of success. Consequently next year I will begin the course with the usual two week section defining history and examining the problems involved in its study, but will follow with a two week section on values and ethics identifying the major concepts with which we are to be dealing. We will then use the rest of the course to apply the ideas introduced in the first four weeks. The unit on ethics should follow Beck's text or at least deal with selections from it. It seems to be the only work which systematically presents ethics in a way useful in the classroom. The reading level is however much too advanced. Even with the relatively advanced groups I taught this year it was necessary to analyze the text almost sentence by sentence in order for students to grasp the meaning. Perhaps the production of a revised edition of that text might be a priority for you. Secondly, materials must be modified for my purposes. Of course this is so because the objectives of the course are largely historical and the moral education materials must mesh rather closely with the historical materials. I do not believe that this problem should rest in your lap. It is my task. Teachers must constantly modify materials of all sorts to fit their goals but the key to successful adaption is understanding. The teacher therefore must have a very firm grounding in ethics, its teaching and potential dangers. Thirdly, my techniques need some modification. I am aware now that much of my style when dealing with moral dilemmas was the result of insecurity. It was cautious. Certain questions plagued me:

1. To what extent can I push a particular point of view to get a reaction?
2. Is the objective I intend achieved or do some students misinterpret the point?
3. To what extent should I question a student to try to discover the reasoning underlying his point of view?
4. To what extent can I expose inconsistencies in a student's moral reasoning or code?
5. To what extent should I attempt to draw out quiet students?

Essentially these questions add up to the following one; at what point does the exercise cease to be constructive and become destructive to the individual student?

With time, practice, and further study I should begin to feel more at home with the subject. However, my doubts raise a serious question. I am by nature a cautious person. I like to think through a course of action before I embark upon it. But what about a more impetuous teacher? What kind of negative effects could his presentation of a moral education unit have on students simply because he did not fully understand the implications of the techniques and materials he was using?

It can be seen by comparing Teacher B to Teacher A, that this teacher is much more reflective about his personal effect on the classroom. Teacher A, in his critical reflections focused on the curricula and on the students' response to it without alluding to his role in the discussions.

Critical Reflections of Observer B

Observer B's reflections on several classroom sessions are worth quoting in detail since they give the reader a flavor of how ethical issues were incorporated into this History teacher's course.

The first session that I observed, the material of which was somewhat atypical for the course, was an attempt to have the students delineate who they thought were 'good' people and who they thought were 'bad' people, and to show that our notions of who is 'good' and 'bad' hinge upon what is valued at the time in society. The teacher presented a dilemma whereby the students had to choose six persons among ten whom they would allow to enter their fallout shelter. The students were asked to break into groups (these usually consisted of four or five students) to reach a unanimous decision as to whom they would let in, and their reasons for choosing each person. The dilemma was staged so that the students would have to choose between people who would be labelled 'good' as defined by our societal values (e.g., a brilliant law student) but were incapable of bearing children, and people who would be defined as immoral in our society (e.g., a pregnant high school dropout) but who were capable of bearing children and therefore ensuring that mankind would survive.

All the groups used a stage three orientation for making their decisions and were adamant that the people who were moral as defined by our society's values should be let in, regardless of the fact that they couldn't have children. The teacher then raised the issue of the need for survival, but the students, while agreeing with the teacher's point of view, were reluctant to change their original decisions. The class ended shortly after the teacher made his point so that the notion that 'what is good and bad can change depending on the circumstances of the situation', was not discussed. However, it appeared that some of the students were a little confused and doubtful of their own decisions at the end of the session, which indicated to me that the teacher had succeeded in giving some of the students a new perspective for judging what is good and bad and succeeded in demonstrating to some that values are more relative than absolute. My only negative feelings about this first session were that only a handful of students participated in both the small group and classroom discussions.

One of the subsequent sessions was devoted to an examination of an excerpt from Machiavelli's *The Prince*. The purpose of the sessions was to aid the students in understanding Machiavelli's philosophy and to demonstrate that his prescription for governmental policy was dictated by his negative view of man's basic nature. The students first read the handout and were then asked to break off into small groups to list the major tenets of his policies on government. After the students had compiled their lists on the blackboard, the teacher questioned the philosophy by raising the issue of 'do any means justify the ends'. To clarify the issue, the teacher asked the students for their opinions as what means justify getting good marks in school (i.e., what about cheating on an exam to get good marks). The students' answers were based largely on stage two, three, and four morality; two or three of the boys stated that they felt cheating was acceptable if you really needed the marks and you didn't get caught, the rest of the class (the girls were most adamant about this) felt that cheating was just not the 'right' thing to do, and one boy based his arguments on stage 5 morality (his protocols on the questionnaire were one of the few that indicated some stage 5 reasoning) stating that cheating in school is wrong because it is breaking the trust that the teacher has for his students. The teacher attempted to clarify the issues by asking the students to set limitations on the 'any means' dilemma and then he tried to relate the discussion back to Machiavelli. No consensus was reached as to the acceptability of Machiavelli's philosophy. The students were unable to come to the conclusion by themselves that Machiavelli's philosophy reflects an attitude that man is basically dishonest and evil, so that the government must deceive the people to stay in power.

The two sessions dedicated to the discussion of Machiavelli were fruitful on the one hand in that the students seemed to grasp the thrust of his philosophy, but were unsuccessful when it came to the students relating the discussion of cheating to Machiavelli's philosophy and relating his prescription for government to his view of man. Once again, only about half the class participated in the discussion.

A later session was used as an introduction to the scientific revolution and was designed to help the students in understanding the moral dilemmas facing the early scientists (this session dealt specifically with Galileo) and to gain an insight into that period of history. The teacher used a case study of a situation parallel to that of Galileo's. The dilemma involved a scientist who lived in a racist society and who had experiments to prove that the two races were equal. If he published his findings slavery would be abolished and the living standards for all classes would decline and chaos would ensue. The class broke up into small groups to discuss the pros and cons of the scientist publishing and to decide what he should do.

The group responses were once again based on stage 2, 3 and 4 morality, with one student (the same student described above) using a stage 5 orientation that slavery is fundamentally wrong and therefore the scientist should accept the consequences and publish as a duty to himself and the society. The discussion ended in conflict between those students who felt he should publish for fame or to abolish slavery and those that felt he should not as he would upset the country or be persecuted. The teacher then asked the students to delineate the categories of responses that the groups had raised (which they did with his guidance) to indicate to the students that there were various ways of looking at the dilemma. Three categories were eventually drawn up—egotistical, others, and principles, and the students attempted to rate the supremacy of reasons, but no consensus was reached. The students' interest and enthusiasm waned at this point so it was left up to the teacher to draw the parallels between the case study and the situation confronting Galileo. The discussion at this session was livelier than usual with more of the students taking part. However, the students lacked the ability to follow through on ideas and to relate the materials.

One of the following sessions focused on the Cold War and its purpose was to aid the students in understanding the cause and reasons for the development and perpetuation of the Cold War. It was also designed to show the students that the way in which the United States and Russia treat each other is a reflection of their attitudes toward man in general. The teacher used a game called the 'Prisoner's Dilemma' to make his point. The game consisted of two teams who play with each other to gain the maximum number of points. The game was constructed so that if each team cooperated with the other they both gained three points; if they tried to beat the other team they gained five points if the other team cooperated (and that team lost three points); if they both tried to beat each other they would both lose three points. Enthusiasm during the game was high although both teams ended up with negative points as a result of trying to beat the other team. The teacher then showed the students how the situation that developed was analagous to the Cold War between the United States and Russia and that the situation continues to exist because the two countries cannot trust each other. Because the students' enthusiasm waned at the end of the game, the final discussion of relating the ideas was left solely to the teacher, and it was difficult to discern whether the students understood the parallels, as they gave no feedback.

The last session to be discussed here consisted of a panel debate between nine members of the class. The topic to be debated was 'the majority has no right to force individuals to accept its standards' versus 'the majority has the right to force individuals to accept its standards'. Each team had prepared evidence to support its position. One team presented constitutional evidence concerning individual rights and freedom to support its position that the majority has no right to force individuals to accept its standards; the other team rebutted by stating that 'throughout history, tragedy has been the result when an individual was allowed to rule the majority'. They used the situation created by Hitler as an example. The debate among the panel members stimulated a great deal of discussion from the rest of the class, with almost three-quarters of the students stating their opinions. During the discussion the teacher acted mainly as a moderator, giving everyone a chance to speak and clarifying issues only when the discussion wandered off topic or when the students seemed confused. While the majority of the class agreed with the 'majority over individual' position, there appeared to be little following through on any one line of reasoning. For example, team I could only refute a team II argument by reciting one of the articles from the constitution. It seemed at times as though they felt the other team was right, but that they had to support their position as they were assigned to it. However, considering that this was the first debate that most of the students had participated in, and that they therefore lacked debating skills, I felt that the session was quite beneficial for the students. It provided the students with an opportunity to reason through and search for evidence to support their position and to defend their arguments against others.

Observer B also tried to tune in on the student discussions with Kohlberg's moral stages. As far as she could hear, most of the discussions focused on stage 3 and 4 arguments with some interjections by a group of boys expressing instrumental hedonistic sentiments (i.e., stage 2). She felt that it was left largely to the teacher to tease out post-conventional principled reasoning from the students' answers and comments. Although observer B did not have the opportunity to post-test these students, her observations at the end of the course are of interest:

Although, even at the end of the course there was little evidence of any spontaneous post-conventional thinking, the students were able to comprehend these high levels of thinking and it appeared that the students often questioned and reassessed their beliefs after thinking about the various alternatives presented. Based on the students' comments over the course of the discussions it appeared to me (although there was no post-testing to validate this) that more of the students were able to comprehend faster and were able to use stage 5 thinking more often when making decisions.

The patterns of communication, according to observer B were predominantly teacher dominated:

In most of the discussions the teacher was the focal point with the students playing only a peripheral role. The typical pattern was a 'teacher to student to teacher' communication process. There was little communication and sharing of ideas among the students themselves. When any 'student to student' communication did take place it appeared that the students talked *at* each other rather than *to* each other and hence were not really listening to each other's ideas. Often it seemed as though the students (usually the few very vocal students) were only interested in relating some of their own personal experiences rather than listening to and thinking about their peers' ideas. I believe that this teacher dominated environment existed due to several factors. Firstly, the students, except during the periods that they broke up into smaller groups, sat in rows facing the teacher at the front. This naturally set up an environment which was conducive to the teacher playing the dominant role and discouraged communication among the students. Secondly, it is my belief (from my observations and from talking to some of the students) that the students did not really consider their peers' comments to be important and therefore directed their comments towards the teacher because they simply were not accustomed to communicating to each other in a classroom situation. In a teacher oriented atmosphere, the students can come to feel that only what the teacher says is important and valid. Also, since the teacher is the one who assigns the students their grades, it is the teacher that they are trying to impress and therefore they direct their answers and remarks towards him. I believe that the students felt this pressure to say what the teacher wanted to hear even when the teacher was trying to elicit the students' feelings and attitudes rather than 'correct' responses. It appeared that this latter situation existed due to the intrinsic nature of traditional classroom settings (i.e., row by row seating, students being evaluated by their teachers and striving for good grades) and also due to the teacher's behavior. While the teacher in-troduced topic matter he was genuinely interested in having the students express their own feelings and ideas, he was also interested in having certain ideas presented to the class. It was understandable that he would want this (in fact this was one of the goals of the course) but this often developed into a guessing game whereby the students would try to guess what the teacher wanted to hear and were then reinforced for giving the 'correct' answer by having their statement written on the board. Perhaps more students could have been encouraged to participate in the discussions if the teacher had really consid-ered and given more support to each student's answers.

Two classroom situations offered more of the students an op-portunity to voice their opinions and allowed for more student oriented discussions. The discussions that took place when the students broke off into small groups were lively and afforded the quieter shy students an opportunity to express themselves under a lower risk condition than that of the total classroom discussion. It appeared that the students felt freer to talk in these small groups as the teacher was not present to evaluate the students, and the quieter students were not intimidated by the louder more aggressive ones (the groups seemed to natu-rally divide into the more vocal students being in the same group). When the small group discussions ended the teacher asked each group to present its ideas and write them on the board for discussion purposes, so that all of the students were equally reinforced. The student seminars were also valuable in that they led to more student oriented discussions. They gave the panel members (each student was a panel member in turn) a chance to act as the resource leaders for the rest of the class. During the debates, the teacher played a minor role, acting as a moderator giving each student a chance to speak and inter-jecting only to clarify terms and issues, to add needed infor-mation, and to develop various principles from the students' comments. Nearly three-quarters of the students participated in these more student-oriented seminars.

Generally then, the classroom sessions consisted mainly of 'teacher-student-teacher' interactions with only a minimal amount of 'student-student' communication. More student oriented discussions were stimulated in the small groups and during the debates. While on the whole, the teacher created an atmosphere that encouraged student participation, a reward system existed that caused some of the shier, less confident students not to participate and created an environment in which the students felt pressure to say the 'right' things.

Summary Evaluation of the Practicum Experience

Teacher B attempted to see his use of "ethical issues" in a History course in light of some contemporary trends in his discipline. He noted that with the advent of H.S. 1 teachers have been faced with the prospect of selling their courses and where previously curricular stress was on skills, now there was a noticeable shift toward the values end of the spectrum. With this trend in mind, he expressed the fear that "moral education" could become a bandwagon in the next few years, "because the materials are so fresh and the cause seemingly, so important". This teacher strongly recommended to us that one of our prime functions should be in the area of teacher education. Specifically he saw our function as familiarizing teachers who intend to present "ethics" in the classroom not only with clear objectives but also to alert them to the potential dangers to students and teachers alike.

Observer B made the following remarks as a general commentary on the practicum and particularly on the course which she observed:

In my opinion the introduction of the experimental moral education program into the regular history course, created a course that was interesting, challenging and of value to the students. I believe that the combination of course material served and achieved three functions. Firstly, the consideration of the moral dilemmas that faced various historical figures and surrounded various historical periods aided the students in gaining a deeper understanding of historical man. The use of contemporary and relevant case studies that drew parallels with past situations, made the course interesting and easier for the students to relate to, and grasp the meaning of historical periods. Secondly, the use of contemporary material to explain the past served to demonstrate to the students that certain moral problems are universal and fundamental. As a result of the understanding of the past and the universality of moral dilemmas, I feel that the students gained a better understanding of contemporary man, the problems that face modern day governments, and of themselves. One example of how the course material achieved these goals simultaneously was the discussion of Machiavelli's philosophy. In order to aid the students in understanding Machiavelli's 'the end justifies the means' philosophy and his resultant prescription for governmental policy, the teacher raised the issue of student cheating and asked the students when, and if, they felt there should be limitations placed on the philosophy. In my opinion this discussion helped the students to understand what Machiavelli was actually saying, to formulate their own opinions on his philosophy, and to understand how they apply these notions themselves in their everyday life.

The frequent use of more remote and less personal material for the discussion (e.g., discussion of who should stay in the fall out shelter rather than a direct discussion of who is moral and immoral) of contemporary moral issues appeared to be valuable in that it provided the students with a chance to express their honest feelings without it being a 'high risk' situation. What I mean by this, is that I feel it is easier for students to express themselves more honestly when they are discussing situations that they can relate to, but yet are not personally involved in. When a student is talking about what 'he (impersonal) should do' rather than about what 'I should do or have done' there is less of a need for the student to conform to his peers or to say things to show the teacher that he or she is a 'good' person.

The only negative aspect that I observed about the use of parallel situations to explain various concepts was that the students found it difficult to relate them, so that it was often left up to the teacher to synthesize the various ideas. For example, while the students enjoyed playing the 'prisoner's dilemma' game, they were unable to spontaneously draw the correspondence between the game situation and the Cold War. However, over the duration of the course, the students improved their ability to do so.

One aspect of the teacher's teaching method that especially contributed to the value of the course, was that he did not try to inculcate the students with what he personally felt was right and wrong. Instead he attempted to have various approaches and perspectives to issues presented to the students, so that they could formulate their own conclusions. He achieved this by drawing out certain ideas, asking questions, and subtly steering the discussion so that the various positions would be exposed. This multidimensional approach was beneficial in that the students were able to assimilate the material presented at their own stage of thinking but were also afforded an opportunity to accommodate to higher levels of reasoning. I feel that this exposure to various stage arguments rather than the imposition of a single view by the teacher was especially important in view of the fact that the students were required to take the course as part of their curriculum. According to Kohlberg's theory this approach was also the most expedient way of reaching all the students and stimulating more developmentally advanced levels of thinking. Although the teacher often rewarded only those students who 'came up' with the position that he wanted presented, his method of proposing several alternatives to problems was good.

One drawback of the course was that the students were given very little time to follow through and develop their own ideas. I felt that if the students had been given the handouts or dilemmas the night before the class and were asked to think about certain issues, then perhaps more meaningful discussions would have taken place, and there would have been less reliance on the teacher to present ideas. One difficulty that the teacher appeared to have with the course was the lack of interesting, challenging, and pertinent material. If this experimental program is to be continued, then perhaps workshops for the teachers should be set up so that ideas and materials could be exchanged.

Overall, I feel that this course was very beneficial both for the students and the teacher. It gave the students an opportunity to discuss important interesting issues in their classroom, and more specifically, it helped the students achieve a deeper understanding of historical and contemporary man, government, freedom, and perhaps gave them new perspective for handling decisions that they personally have to make. If nothing else, it demonstrated to the students that there is seldom one absolute answer or view to an issue, but rather there are several alternatives upon which to base decisions and judgments. I feel that the course made the teacher more aware of the fact that his students are at different levels in their thinking and the need to really listen to the students to detect what level they are reasoning at. In addition I feel the course made him more aware of the moral dimensions of education and his own classroom behavior. My only apprehension about a course in moral education is that it may turn into a course whereby a teacher moralizes and tries to proselytize his students to accept his own personal ideas. If teachers are made aware of this danger, and if moral education 'courses' are incorporated into other school programs (as opposed to strict moral education courses) then a course of the nature I observed could be of great value in our educational system.

It should be noted that observer B raises very similar points that observer A did in her summary analysis.

SCHOOL C

The Teacher-Observer Pair

Teacher C was a part-time student enrolled in the Master's program in the Department of Curriculum. She had taught high school social studies for several years but was not teaching at the time of enrollment because of child rearing responsibilities. She had made an arrangement with one of her former colleagues to take his social studies class on a part time basis for her practicum teaching. Her background in this area consisted of several courses related to "Ethics" at the Institute.

Observer C was a full time female Ph.D. candidate in the Department of History and Philosophy. She had several courses related to moral philosophy and her interest in this practicum was for applied experience in moral education.

Description of the School and Students

School C was a suburban school and could be characterized as middle class. The class consisted of 24 grade 11 and 12 students who were taking a course labelled "Man and Society". This class was normally taught by a young male teacher and our teacher only took the class on a part time basis. Teacher C was not perceived as the regular teacher and the teaching situation here was far from ideal for the purposes of the practicum. Teacher C only taught for a period of 3 1/2 weeks since the regular teacher already had established a schedule of topics for these students. This regular teacher attended many classes of teacher C and his presence was believed to have an effect on how the class would act with the prac-

Table 4

Objectives for Social Studies Units

Objectives

AIMS: 1. To get a student to distinguish among the various ways in which a situation can be viewed; i.e., morally, politically, legally, religiously, economically, etc.

   2. To get a student to understand what is meant by moral point of view and to understand his moral point of view, see its consequences and limitations and evolve it towards a more operable view.

   3. To inculcate good discussion skills.
      a) reach some agreement as to the nature of the issues raised in the dilemma.
      b) search out all relevant facts.
      c) discuss various solutions to the dilemma.
      d) discuss the limitations of the various solutions and propose amendments to solve them.
      e) become aware that it is not always possible to arrive at one fixed solution because of disagreement on basic principles, i.e., the value of human life.
      f) present other points of view on the dilemma if they have not been raised, i.e., the legal viewpoint and their relation to the moral points of view being discussed.
      g) stress the responsibility that everyone has for his moral point of view.

   4. Written skills: to take a moral dilemma and write up a workable hypothesis citing the principles used in coming to this conclusion. To be able to support all generalities with appropriate facts and beliefs.

ticum teacher. From the first author's brief observation of this teacher, our impression of his style was that of a warm authoritarian leader. He seemed quite different in personal style from teacher C.

Description of Course Content

Teacher C had several objectives in mind which she delineates as follows in Table 4.

Several topics were discussed in her classes namely, abortion, euthanasia, the moral point of view and poverty. Teacher C made lesson plans for these topics and drew from the following materials:

1) *Human Life and the State.* OISE Publication, John Eisenberg, 1972.

2) *Things I Cannot Change.* A film on Poverty produced by the National Film Board of Canada.

Regarding alterations in the materials she notes:

> I stuck to the materials I cited above; however, the case studies on abortion and enthanasia raised so many issues that the students eventually got discouraged when no right answer appeared possible. Also, the materials tended to illicit a 'gut' response from the student rather than a reasoned response.

The outline of her lesson plan on abortion is in Table 5.

Critical Reflections of Teacher C

Teacher C was quite different from Teacher A in regard to the use of home assignments. She gave four home assignments. To her, they were an attempt to discover what each student felt about the issues raised and the reasons for his viewpoint. The assignment also gave her an opportunity to point out to each student inconsistencies and consequences which issued from their viewpoints. She noted that in several cases, the student's written viewpoint differed radically from his viewpoint in class.

Teacher C reflects on her overall teaching style as follows:

> My type of teaching requires a fair amount of time before it shows success. I like to begin the discussion and then turn it over to the students. This is only possible when they have learned to listen attentively to one another, understand the various points of view and care enough to challenge one another about them. I ran into difficulty because the class was used to the devil's advocate approach where a teacher throws out controversial statements guaranteed to arouse the most apathetic student. However, some classes were beginning to become more thoughtful and attentive, but the class still seemed reluctant to take the effort to seriously consider what one another was saying.

Table 5

Session Plan on Abortion

I. *Goals*

    a) to set down the law on abortion and discuss its consequences with respect to
      i) the rights of the mother
      ii) the rights of the child.

    b) discuss why the exact definition of what endangers or is likely to endanger a mother's health is left deliberately vague.

    c) why it is easier to get abortions in some hospitals than others.

    d) why the law does not define the nature of the foetus.

    e) give the class two definitions of the nature of a foetus and see the consequences of each definition for the mother, the unborn child, society, the existing law.

II. *Law and Abortion*

If a person is to procure an abortion, the request must be presented to a committee chosen by each hospital's Board of Directors. This committee decides on the basis of whether or not the birth of the child or the continuation of pregnancy would endanger or be likely to endanger the mother's life or health.

1. According to the law, what are the rights of the mother?

2. What are the rights of the unborn child?

3. Interpret this law so that June would have been allowed to have an abortion.

4. Interpret this law so that June would not be allowed to have an abortion.

5. Why has the law not spelled out exactly what is meant by danger to the mother's health and life? What are the advantages of this deliberate vagueness? What are the disadvantages of this deliberate vagueness?

6. Why does the law not define the nature of the foetus? Where does the law place the responsibility for defining the nature of the foetus?

III. *Two Descriptions of the Nature of the Foetus*

1. The foetus is a living being with a human potentiality at conception; therefore, it must be treated with human dignity.

   a) What is the basic right of every foetus? If the foetus is abnormal in some way, does this alter its right to be treated with human dignity?

   b) Whose responsibility is it to protect the rights of the foetus? mother's, father's, society's, anyone else's?

   c) How does this definition affect the rights of the mother, the father?

   d) How does this definition affect the present law on abortion?

   e) According to this definition, what would the mother be doing if she had an abortion, the doctor if he performed an abortion?

   f) What changes would you make in this description of the foetus?

2. A foetus is a parasitic cellular growth in the uterus and as such is completely under the control of the mother.

   a) What is the basic right of the foetus according to this definition? Why?

   b) What is the mother's prime responsibility? the father's? society's?

   c) What are the rights of the mother according to this definition? rights of the father?

   d) How does this description of the foetus affect the present law on abortion?

   e) According to this definition, what would the mother be doing if she had an abortion, the doctor, if he performed an abortion?

   f) What changes would you make in this definition of the foetus?

IV. *Homework*

1. How would you define the nature of a foetus?

2. Draw up a law on abortion that best reflects your view on the issue.

I also had the students work in groups and then present their findings to the class. This method worked very well.

The practicum raised many questions in the mind of this teacher as to the problems encountered in dealing with value issues in the schools:

I still have not arrived at any definite view as to whether or not schools should provide a class in values.

Observer C and I discovered that students have great difficulty in understanding exactly what is meant by values, although they discuss issues in value-laden terms all the time. Many students believe, for example, that values have their origin in religion or in rules and are imposed on them from outside. To create your own moral framework is a very alien notion to most of them. The other problem that I confronted was the peer group morality. For example, the peer group morality felt that abortion was every woman's right. Many students conformed to this belief even though it conflicted with their personal views.

The next problem was my own morality. It is very hard to conduct a class in values because your own attitude cunningly declares itself in your tone of voice or your facial expression. How does a teacher remain impartial? If it is impossible to remain impartial, then, should a teacher declare his beliefs and prejudices on every issue as it comes up?

However, in spite of these problems, I feel very strongly that there is a need to have some attention paid to morals so that every student can make some attempt to discover the nature of his values, and the implications of these beliefs for himself and for society. It is also crucial that he see the inherent contradictions in his attitude and try and correct them. Finally, he should see that in our pluralistic society there is no right and wrong that is the same for everyone. All these objectives must be pursued if he is to become a honest, fair and compassionate person.

Although a class in values might be helpful, my emphasis is still on the teacher. Every subject has a value dimension. Therefore, every teacher should have some training in value education. This has to be done at the teacher training level.

Values are too important an issue to restrict to one class. Also, teachers should be aware of their moral viewpoint and its limitations.

Critical Reflections of Observer C

Observer C administered Kohlberg's moral judgment instrument at the beginning of the units which Teacher C conducted. Consistent with our other high school samples, these students were reasoning at stages 2, 3 and 4, with stage 3 clearly the recurrent stage throughout the protocols. There were four protocols with a global 3 score, six with a global 3(2), four with a global 3(4), and two with a global 4(3). Five of the protocols resulted in no global score, though in each case stages 3 and 4 were legitimate minor stages and often very close to being a dominant stage. The other three protocols scored 3(5), 2(4), and 5.

The scoring results indicated dominant but transitional stage 3 thinking among the students. Only four were pure stage 3 with about half of the others responding at stage 2 and half at stage 4 as minor stages. There were two protocols in which post-conventional thinking was significant. One was a mixture of 3 and 5 while the other was nearly all stage 5 and 6.

Observer C notes a discrepancy between protocol responses and class responses:

> Though protocol results demonstrated predominant stage 3 thinking among class members, students' classroom responses proved to be quite different. Participation in class discussion was often good but a strong peer group stage 2 morality was evident. Very seldom were stage 3 reasons voiced in class and the occasional stage 4 thinking was brutally squashed. As might be expected, the post-conventional students withdrew completely from involvement.

> There are several reasons for this circumstance. From a theoretical standpoint it could be expected that transitional stage 3 thinkers, when dealing with heavy personal issues such as euthanasia and abortion, would revert to strong stage 2 reasons and in fact, scoff at stage 4 reasons (not being very firmly entrenched at stage 3 or 4).

Possibly a more important reason is that the class had been accustomed to a teacher (Mr. X) who commonly used the devil's advocate method in dealing with class discussion topics. The group quite early picked up on Mrs. Y's (Teacher C) 'liberal' bias and seemed to voice hedonistic reasons, as if to play devil's advocate to her. On more than one occasion I overheard students refer to her bias ('She feels sorry for all those poor people').

From the start a kind of bravado atmosphere was observed in this class. As stated previously, such a climate stemmed more from Mr. (X's) influence than Mrs. (Y's) but its effects lingered once she took over, thus affecting her use of the materials. However, self-centered, hedonistic talk strikes me as common among young people in general and not peculiar to this class. Kids in their mid-teens frequently make remarks like 'I have to think about myself. . .', 'feeling sorry for the poor isn't going to get you anywhere', 'it's not fair to the rest of society for some people not to work', or 'if there were no restrictions, I'd shoplift', and so on. It is apparently more acceptable to say such things than to appeal to niceness or the need for law and order—only squares think that way.

As further evidence of the discrepancy between classroom responses and actual sentiments, Mrs. Y reported that students' written assignments correlated more closely with their protocols than their classroom comments.

Flow of communication between teacher and students was complicated by the fact that Mrs. Y was a temporary visiting teacher to the class. But that was not the only reason the communication was not entirely successful. One significant problem was using the case study approach. Mrs. Y had organized the course with nearly total use of case studies (written, filmed and taped). Class discussion usually centered around drawing out relevant facts in the case but often disintegrated into probing individual students regarding 'what would you do if you were June Jacobsen?' Through putting the students on the spot in this manner communication was weakened as well as privacy invaded. Euthanasia, abortion, shoplifting and even poverty (for lower middle income children who feel threatened by the poor) were emotion-laden topics for these students. My observations were discussed with Mrs. Y, who agreed to try to objectify the material more. It was suggested that she tease out various moral positions on certain issues without advocating one or another. We also discussed trying to get students to identify a moral problem as different (and in what ways) from other problems, such as economic ones. My point was that the students needed some understanding of the terminology before being able to deal with case studies on any level other than an emotional one.

Summary Evaluation of the Practicum Experience

Since both Teacher C and Observer had similar summary evaluations we will quote only observer C here.

Apart from the day to day operation of the practicum, the observation time helped me solidify some thoughts on value education programs for public schools and in general. The following recommendations reflect a great deal of deliberation and are still being contemplated: value education programs should be voluntary, not part of any compulsory curriculum; case studies should be combined with other kinds of materials, never used alone; teachers of value programs must have good background in the theory and scoring before teaching a class.

It is the latter recommendation that troubles me the most, for the teacher I observed had much training in theory and scoring, yet still her personal sentiments were obvious through tone of voice, priorities in questioning, choice of case studies, and the like. Teacher dominance and influence is a strong force in any classroom and particularly dangerous when the topic is values, ethics, morality or whatever. Given the nature of the subject and the potential influence of teachers, I do not think it appropriate to be a compulsory course.

There was a time during the practicum in which I considered writing a paper entitled 'Is It Ethical to Teach Ethics'? as my final statement for the course. It was to reflect my growing concern with the impossibility of teaching about values without perpetrating a value system. I continue to doubt that values can be totally objectified, but I have come to see certain formats as acceptable: teaching some moral terminology (what is a value? how does it differ from a goal?), helping students to recognize a moral problem and a moral reason (as different from, say, an economic one), and teaching awareness of various ways to look at a moral problem (hedonistic, religious, rational). Perhaps, in a pluralistic society, tolerance (not necessarily acceptance) is an important factor.

GENERAL CONCLUSIONS

We are well aware of the problem of generality concerning some of the conjectures we are about to make concerning our experience with the practicum. Keeping in mind that the practicum was exploratory and in the pilot stage it nevertheless raises issues and questions for future work in this area.

All participants in the practicum including the teacher (Sullivan) saw necessary changes in format for future practicum of this nature. The spacing of the observation periods once a week caused discontinuity in the observation attempts. In the future observation will be done in blocs of time so that there will be a continuity in the observations. In other words, instead of spacing 13 observation periods over a period of thirteen weeks, there might be 10 observation periods over a period of two weeks.

It also seems important to have good rapport develop between the teacher-observer team. This allows for an open critical atmosphere for all involved and can only add to the merit of the practicum where reciprocal feedback seems most essential.

It was suggested by one observer that the teachers in the practicum should participate in the scoring workshop. In the practicum just completed, the teachers did not attend the scoring workshop on Kohlberg's moral judgment scale. Observer A felt that the workshop deepened her knowledge of cognitive-developmental moral theory and she thought that the teachers might likewise benefit by it even though they would not be involved in testing and scoring the protocols. Her feeling was that the workshop would enhance the teacher's ability to follow different levels of moral discourse in class.

As would be expected from our normative data quoted in chapter 1 figure 3 and chapter 4 figure 7 our students' modal stage was 3 (i.e., Good-Boy Nice-Girl) with elements of other stages operating. There were few post-conventional responses observed in all classes that we worked in. It should also be noted that all of our observers commented on the reticence to speak up of all post-conventional students that they observed in class. Although stage 3 thinking was the modal stage for all classes, two of our observers noted that stage 2 thinking tended to be very boisterous and had a tendency to carry the class along with them, at least temporarily. This dramatizes the importance for support of other points of view in the class, but the questions arises as to whether the teacher should come right out and support the use of stage 5 thinking (Kohlberg's notion of cognitive conflict did not prevail here because our stage 5 students were reticent to venture their point of view).

Another important observation seemed to be consistent across all three observers and that was the marked *teacher-centered* format of all the classes as a rule. We do not mean to criticize a teacher-centered format but it may not and probably is not the best format for classes that are interested in moral issues. It tends to put the teacher in a position of authority which could discourage autonomous exploration by the students. In one instance (i.e., teacher A) it seemed that the teacher was totally unaware of the fact that this was his dominant class format. This was true to a somewhat lesser extent of the other teachers. Observer A suggested that in the future practicum, the teachers should be acquainted with several alternative formats or groupings which he could implement for discussion purposes. It may be profitable to video tape some teaching sessions so that the teacher will have his own class as feedback. A teacher-centered format has a tendency to let discussion center on issues raised by the teacher since he remains the center of attention, and his authority is built into the very framework of the school. Observer B noted a difference when Teacher B moved to a debate format. She noted that in the two classes where the "debate" format was implemented there was a marked increase in students voicing their own opinions and student oriented discussion. No doubt one could also criticize the debate format, but the point we wish to make here is simply that with rare exceptions, any high school classes are entrenched in a teacher-centered format which may not be the most viable format for high-school students in their discussion of moral issues and problems. As observer B put it, the teacher-centered format created an environment in which the students felt the pressure to say the "right things".

The question of the appropriateness of topics was also raised by the practicum participants. Two of our teachers encountered difficulties and some embarrassment while dealing with the topic of "abortion". From our point of view it is difficult to say why one topic will be appropriate and another will not. The fact that a topic is controversial should not constitute a reason for not covering a topic. Perhaps what is most important here is that the students be given some options as to what topics are to be discussed. In the two instances where abortion was discussed, the topic was unilaterally introduced by the teachers. We will discuss this issue more generally in our final chapter under the topic of indocrination.

In conclusion, we can tentatively say that a practicum in moral education seems to be of critical use for teachers interested in subjects where ethical issues are discussed. All of the participants in the practicum, (teachers and observers alike) strongly recommended that teacher training in the teachers' colleges should critically explore the ethical dimensions of the curriculum. In view of their own experiences, these teachers and observers were cautious about introducing full scale moral education in the Ontario schools with the present facilities of teacher training institutions.

VI

Retrospect and Prospect: Issues and Questions Generated by the Moral Education Project

At this point we would like to make some critical reflections on moral education. Although our project is modest in its scope and objectives, it nevertheless gives us a concrete base from which more general reflections can be tendered. As noted earlier, the origin of this project was based on interdisciplinary discussions at the Ontario Institute focusing on the role of values in the school. These informal discussions led to a more formal conference on moral education where several prominent scholars across several disciplines addressed themselves to questions related to moral education in the schools. Subsequent to this conference the Mackay Report on Moral and Religious Education in Ontario was published and the body of the report reflected a strong influence from some of our conference papers. This report encouraged experimental programs to be carried out at the Ontario Institute for Studies in Education which might bear on present and future perspectives in the area of value education. Our project is just one of several at the Institute which addresses itself to some of the issues and questions raised by that report. The project has been multifocused from its beginnings. In addition to its interdisciplinary focus, the project personnel have been involved in a) applied programmes in moral education at the elementary and secondary school levels, b) problems in evaluation of programmes in moral education, c) short term workshops for teachers and administrators interested in moral education and finally d) teacher-training in value laden subjects. The aims of our project have been modest and because of the small number of people we have worked with we recognize the limitations on what we can say in any one of the areas in which we have been involved. Nevertheless, we can say that we have been systematic in our attack on the problems we have tackled and we have always tried to critically evaluate our on-going work. This report is a critical summary of our work to date. On the basis of the previous chapters we would like to conclude our study with a reflection on some broader issues on which our project has some bearing. We will divide our discussion into four major areas:

a) A critical perspective on Kohlberg's cognitive-developmental approach to moral education.

b) The discussion of controversial issues in the schools.

c) The place of moral education in the curriculum.

d) The relationships between the school and community in the wider moral perspective.

a) *Kohlberg's Cognitive-Developmental Perspective in Moral Education*

It seems appropriate at this point to put the work of Kohlberg and colleagues (Kohlberg, 1971) in perspective insofar as this theory has contributed to our efforts. It is clear by the tables and graphs discussed throughout this book that this theory has had no small influence on our thinking. Kohlberg's work must be looked at critically because of the theory's intense popularity at this time in educational circles. We have reviewed elsewhere, in relation to Piaget's work, the problems of uncritically extrapolating a psychological theory into an educational context (Hunt and Sullivan, 1973, Sullivan, 1967, Sullivan, 1969).

Kohlberg's writing (1971) has emphasized that the form of moral reasoning can be separated from its content. He draws from this position the possibility of teaching or stimulating the formal aspects of moral reasoning which he claims enables his perspective to sidestep the problem of indoctrination of specific moral content. The Mackay Report has essentially accepted this point of view. However, it has been argued by several moral philosophers that the separation of form and content in moral reasoning is not so simple a task and that the problem of indocrination is not so easily sidestepped (see Beck, Crittenden and Sullivan, 1971, Crittenden, 1972). Our own work has not been based on Kohlberg's position on this issue because our experiences have left us with the conclusion that the subtle form-content distinction made by Kohlberg is an untested assumption rather than an unquestioned reality. We therefore do not follow Kohlberg or the Mackay Report's position that possibility of moral indoctrination is eliminated by the form-content distinction. We will argue later that problems related to indocrination can be dealt with in other ways that are more practically feasible.

Kohlberg (1971) has also argued for the primacy of Justice as the overriding principle for the moral point of view. Along with this he posits that his stages and their end point (i.e., Justice) are universal to all cultures. There is a tendency in Kohlberg's writing to over-extend the claims for his stage theory. We are not here arguing against the validity of his stages; rather, we are questioning the lengths to which he extends the principle of Justice as the overriding superordinate principle. Without denying the possibility of his stages we wonder if he has captured only one facet of the moral reasoning process, albiet a compelling one. R.S. Peters (1971) reflects a similar concern:

> It may well be that some generalizations have been established about certain aspects of moral development, but these may be peculiar to the limited range of phenomena studied. It would be unfortunate if these generalizations were erected into a general theory of moral development without account being taken of the differences exhibited by the phenomena that have not been studied. (p. 237)

It is important to keep in mind that Kohlberg is exploring a particular aspect of the moral world which is reflected by certain historical moral philosophical positions to the relative exclusion of others (see Murdock, 1962). Although other perspectives are present, one cannot help but see the strong influence of Kant, liberal social contract theory and contemporary English analytic philosophy to the exclusion of most systems of ethics that have as their basis a transcendent religious perspective. Crittenden (1972) emphasizes the possibility that even if one was in agreement with Kohlberg's position it should be recognized that this commits you to one interpretation of morality and to certain moral beliefs in preference to others. In more specific terms:

> Whatever conceptual relationships exist between 'justice' and 'morality', we cannot advance very far in our discussion of justice without examining its connection with what are commonly taken to be other moral values, in particular, freedom, equality, and fraternity (although the last has been rather neglected in liberal moral theory). The connections are often worked out in the context of the doctrine of natural rights. In his interpretation of justice, Kohlberg acknowledges the doctrine of general human rights and affirms the belief that all human beings, despite their differing capacities and merits have equal human worth. These beliefs are of course common to several contemporary moral systems (e.g., liberal, socialist, Christian). Yet the notion of justice still varies in important respects from one system to another and its role in the perception and resolution of moral questions is different. Apart from other factors, the relative emphasis given to the ideals of freedom, equality, and fraternity invariably makes a difference to the interpretation of justice. (Crittenden, 1972, p. 18)

In light of the Mackay Report's uncritical extrapolation of Kohlberg's theory into an educational context, it is important to bear in mind another point that Crittenden (1972) has made:

> In the foregoing comments, although I have been pointing to what I believe are inadequacies in Kohlberg's moral theory, my main purpose has been to stress that it is in fact only one moral theory and it does carry with it committments on the content of moral beliefs and judgments. It is a version of morality in which the 'extension' of our moral judgments includes every human being, treated as having equal human worth. It restricts morality to the range of concepts (such as rights, obligation, duty) associated with justice and interprets morality as an instrument for achieving human welfare. It involves the rejection of various positions that make some claim to be moral as, for example, moral conventionalism, religiously based morality, any system that builds in morally relevant differences between human beings at the ground floor, any system that appeals to absolute moral standards (the view that

there are certain actions one is never justified in doing regardless of the consequences). Thus, even if the moral position
Kohlberg takes were thought to be most satisfactory, it would
be a serious mistake for public schools to accept it on the assumption that it was independent of all moral content and
settled nothing one way or the other about different moral
beliefs and systems. (p. 23)

In view of the reservations we are making about Kohlberg's
theory, it seems necessary to explain the context in which we use
him in our own work. First of all, we have found Kohlberg's instrument for the assessment of moral judgment the most sophisticated and reliable instrument that psychological assessment de-
vices have to offer. The instrument can be reliably scored and its
validity is argued within the perspective of cognitive developmental
theory. Although its major focus is on moral reasoning, this limi-
tation may be an advantage. We would argue that the school
should be interested in the processes of the students' moral reasoning, notwithstanding other important factors. The reason why we
have not used other instruments to date is simply that we have not
found any others that are satisfactory to our purposes.

Secondly, because of the broad age spans with which we have
worked we find that Kohlberg's developmental perspective has
been most helpful in its orientation. His developmental stage
norms have given the whole area of moral philosophy a new slant
which incorporates and improves the seminal contributions of Piaget's original work on moral judgment. As a psychological
theorist, Kohlberg logically extends what Piaget sees as the psychologist's contribution to the moral domain:

The moral philosopher discusses values or norms as such, and
they do not, of course, concern the psychologist. But in studying individual subjects, the latter verifies that they take as
givens or recognize norms, whence a series of problems. What
are the norms of the subject? By what processes does the subject come to feel that he is bound by them? Are these processes the same at every age or do they change? etc. (Piaget,
1971, p. 194)

Kohlberg's developmental stage norms and our own Canadian
replications of these norms argue for the continued viability of this

kind of approach. We have argued elsewhere about the importance of taking a developmental approach in dealing with educational problems (Ausubel and Sullivan, 1970; Hunt and Sullivan, 1973; Sullivan, 1968, 1969). In our own work we have been interested in developmental change which can be seen in the ways we have tried to assess our project. For example, in our classroom work we have always tried to pre-test at the beginning of the course and give two follow up assessments. The first follow up was at the end of the course and the second one a year later (see figures 4, 5, 6 and 7). We have already indicated that in our own classroom work we have utilized Kohlberg's model in order to get a general idea of our students' levels and stages of moral reasoning. This is a helpful guide to what kinds of discussion will be appropriate for the students (see especially Beck, 1971). As seen from our own normative findings, most of our eleventh and twelfth grade students reason at the conventional level with a mixture of stage three and stage four thinking. There is also some stage two and five orientation. One of our objectives for high school students is to encourage post-conventional thinking since we think that students in high school have the cognitive capacities to reason beyond conventional levels of thinking. When the programme was being applied to the elementary school, "conventional" moral stages would be one of our objectives since many of the students would be developmentally at the pre-moral level à la Kohlberg. In other words, our objectives varied because we are *developmentally* oriented and we use in our evaluative framework a *developmental* theory (see Hunt and Sullivan, 1973).

b) *The Discussion of Controversial Issues in the Schools*

It is often assumed that when we enter a "controversial" area such as values, religion, civics, or the like a different set of educational norms applies. A teacher must place less emphasis on instruction or perhaps more, and must be less authoritarian or perhaps more. There is some disagreement about what precisely the difference should be, but widespread agreement that there should be a difference (Beck, 1974).

From our own work we would propose that educational norms and procedures should not change when one moves to a so-called "controversial" field, except in the usual way that approaches vary from one field of education to another. There is no more (and no less) reason to enforce and "indoctrinate" in physics than in morals.

The notion of a controversial area is, of course, difficult to pin down. To some people it is still a controversial question whether or not man in any sense evolved from other forms of animal life, whereas to other people the occurrence of a process of evolution of some kind is so uncontroversial that it can simply be assumed in a biology or anthropology course. To some people all value questions are controversial, whereas to other people there is a clear necessity to distinguish between controversial and non-controversial value questions. These differences of viewpoint often occur along community lines, so something that is controversial in one community is not in another (Beck, 1974).

We assume that a controversial area is one in which the great majority of important statements and attitudes one might express could seriously and legitimately be questioned, within the community or communities one has in mind. It will be seen, as we progress, that on this conception the distinction between controversial and non-controversial areas is greatly diminished. For there are many propositions in physics, for example, that should be seriously questioned but are taken for granted; and many propositions in morals, for example, that need not be seriously questioned (except insofar as *any* proposition in any field should be questioned) but that pass unnoticed by people who make generalizations about controversial areas.

It would be more appropriate from our standpoint, then, if this section were entitled: "Education in areas that are *commonly assumed* in our society to be strongly and distinctively controversial." For we wish to question this assumption. But whatever one's view on this issue may be, the category of "controversial areas" provides a good starting point for consideration of a particularly interesting group of educational problems and subject fields. One of the problems salient to moral education is the issue of indoctrination in the schools.

The Problem of Indoctrination. What do we mean when we say there is a problem of indoctrination? It may certainly be more effective, in some sense, to inject new information and ideas into the discussion, and to spend time in thorough consideration of general principles. But does this not endanger the autonomy of the student? Surely controversial areas are ones in which effectiveness is not an issue. Should not our concern be the natural, free growth of the student toward his own distinctive set of opinions?

This objection raises rather clearly the issue of just what we mean by indoctrination. Are we to accept the assumption that the effective presentation of ideas by a teacher—often his own ideas—in a controversial area constitutes indoctrination and therefore is unacceptable? Are we to accept the assumption that reference to a particular moral theory (e.g., Kohlberg's) is inherently indoctrinative? Let us begin by reviewing some of the observations made in recent years by analytic philosophers concerning the nature of indoctrination.

A careful look at the dictionary meanings of the term indoctrination indicates that its historical meanings were not pejorative (Crittenden, 1973). It is only in contemporary philosophical thought that this term has taken on negative connotations. Beck (1974) in a recent summary of the philosophical literature on this topic indicates that this literature reveals a fairly general agreement that indoctrination is a bad thing, but less agreement about what precisely makes it bad. John Wilson has maintained that inculcation of ideas is indoctrinative if the *content* of what is being taught is mistaken or uncertain. R.M. Hare rejects this aspect of Wilson's analysis and maintains, rather, that indoctrination is distinguished chiefly by the *aim* of the indoctrinator, namely, that of preventing the person being indoctrinated from ever thinking rationally about the issues in question. He feels that it is sometimes necessary to inculcate ideas—in young children, for example—but that such inculcation should not be described as indoctrination if it is being done out of worthy motives and if the intention is eventually to replace the unquestioning acceptance with a reflective, critical acceptance (or non-acceptance). Yet others have maintained the more commonsense view that indoctrination is taking place when beliefs are being induced in a *manner* such that the critical faculties of the person being indoctrinated are not engaged (Crittenden, 1973; Morris, 1966). In this context, Crittenden (1973) maintains that:

> . . . regardless of whether a certain teaching activity might be judged to be miseducational, it is not even a candidate for the title of 'indoctrination' unless the teacher is trying to inculcate beliefs that form a more or less systematic body of doctrine, and have implications for human conduct. Then, given this kind of content, teaching is 'indoctrination' when it is miseducational under either of the following aspects: (i) If the teacher presents the specified content in a way that violates the epistemic criteria of the appropriate mode of inquiry —makes unwarranted claims, confuses literal descriptions of phenomena with mythic or metaphoric interpretations, etc.; (ii) If the teacher's method or manner is such that under the circumstances one may reasonably expect a false understanding to result (the student has to be in a position to recognize relevant and adequate reasons for what the teacher is trying to get him to believe). (p. 111)

Finally, a fourth position is that content, aim and manner are not particularly important; the crucial question is the *result* of the whole process: does the indoctrinated person have a worse quality of life and mind than he had before the indoctrination took place (Tate, 1970)?

It seems rather obvious that there is some truth in all of these positions. The term "indoctrination" is basically a value word, and has reference to a fairly wide range of bad types of inculcation. False content, unworthy aims, mindless methods, and unfortunate results are all to be avoided, and in classical cases of indoctrination they are all to be found together. But there are less typical cases of indoctrination where, for example, the content is sound but the method is indoctrinative; or the aim and method are indoctrinative but in fact no characteristically indoctrinative state of mind results. In these cases we are less inclined to talk of indoctrination having taken place, although in a certain sense it has.

The important point about these definitional exercises is not that they have captured for us the "essense" of indoctrination. Rather it is that they have displayed before us more clearly than before a number of things to be on guard against in education:

peddling false beliefs; adopting authoritarian, inculcative intentions with respect to students; using methods that do not engage the free spirit and critical faculties of students; and producing in students a state of mindless acceptance of conventional attitudes and beliefs (Beck, 1974).

Now, in employing the theoretical discussion method which allows a teacher to introduce new ideas and argue his own point of view, are we being indoctrinative in any of these ways? Is it true that in our zeal for effectiveness we are hindering the natural, free growth of the student? And if we are, is it wrong to do so?

Several comments are appropriate here. First, it is difficult to see how the introduction of new information and ideas necessarily detracts from the student's freedom to adopt his own preferred set of opinions. Indeed, it may increase his range or choices. This depends upon the manner in which the new material is introduced. A teacher who is determined to be non-authoritarian can allow a free atmosphere while at the same time introducing new material (and even giving an indication of his own views about values).

Second, there is such a thing as "group indoctrination," and so-called free group discussion can be as indoctrinative for a particular student as any program of moralizing administered by a teacher (against whom the student may have long since learned to be on guard). New information and ideas from outside sources, whether transmitted through the teacher, through books and films, or through obviously knowledgeable and innovative students in the class, may be the only means whereby a particular student is able to rise above the pressures of his peer group and achieve autonomy in thought and action.

Finally, it is a mistake to assume that controversial areas are distinctive in such a way that in *their* case "effectiveness is not an issue." This could be so only if controversial questions were entirely relative, or if they were unimportant. Obviously they are not unimportant; indeed progress in the solution of controversial value problems, for example, would seem to be among the most important objectives of human endeavor in the present age. But are controversial questions entirely relative? Some philosophers in the present century have argued that value questions are, that there is no right answer to a value question, or that whatever a man thinks is right, is right; and this view seems to have been accepted by many people, at least as something to which they pay lip service. In practice, however, we find that this view is absurd; people do puzzle over value questions, obviously assuming that some answers are better than others; people do take facts into account, obviously assuming that they are relevant to value questions. And it is clear, from many considerations, that these assumptions are correct: in various important ways, value questions do admit of objective inquiry. It would seem, then, that we should be concerned about effectiveness in controversial areas as in all other areas of the curriculum.

What is needed is a subtle combination of injecting new ideas (from various sources) into the discussion, on the one hand; and allowing scope for members of the group to reject these ideas (in part or in whole) and to propose alternatives, on the other. We are convinced that such a combination is possible, but only experience can show precisely how to strike the right balance. Unfortunately, in education systems run on broadly authoritarian lines, the necessary relationship of mutual trust, respect and cooperation among students and teachers is extremely difficult to cultivate. One may easily be *forced* into indoctrination by the authority structure within which one expresses one's views.

There are many things that a teacher in an authoritarian school can do to help create the appropriate environment for group discussion in his own classroom. To begin with, he can learn to have intellectual humility, being willing immediately to admit ignorance, acknowledge a mistake, or modify his views in the face of sound counter-arguments. The teacher should not pose as an intellectual genius or as an infallible source of knowledge. There are considerable pressures upon him from parents, the public and even students to maintain such a pose, but he must resist them. In particular, he must learn to give full acknowledgement to and encourage full expression of, the expertise of his students in particular areas. Only in this way can a spirit of cooperative search for knowledge and wisdom be developed in the classroom.

In general, a teacher should show respect for students as persons. Permissiveness is not what is needed; we are only "permissive" to inferiors. What is needed is that the teacher treat students as other people, who have a diversity of abilities and desires (just as he has), and with whom he happens to be engaged in certain semipersonal cooperative activities. He has been given a degree of authority, put forward as a resource person, chairman, leader; but he should exercise these roles only insofar as the group as a whole is convinced that it is necessary for the cooperative activities in which they are engaged.

It is in these ways, then, rather than in adopting an artificial and ineffectual "hands off" policy, that the solution to the problem of indoctrination in controversial areas lies. Teachers will always exercise some influence over students, just as students will exercise influence over teachers and fellow students. This is how it must be. However, if the influence is exercised with good intentions and with due regard for general problems of evidence and proof, and if the personality of the other party is fully engaged and his individuality and autonomy is fully respected, any charge of indoctrination will be difficult to sustain.

Teacher Training. Is there a necessity for teacher training in areas related to moral education? The answer to this question from looking at our project is an unqualified *yes*. All of the teachers and observers in our practicum stressed the importance of serious reflection in the teacher training colleges in all areas of the curriculum which are value laden. From our work we conclude that the range of the previous statement covers most subjects in the curriculum. Our practicum participants stressed the importance of moral dimensions in such varied topics as history, social studies and comparative religion. No doubt this stress can be seen in other subjects (e.g., Humanities, literature, etc.).

Using Kohlberg's stages as a guide, for a moment, let us reflect on some issues that might be related to secondary education. We have already indicated that there is a selective process in education and ordinarily teachers who are successful in professional educational circles have conventional moral values. This is not necessarily an indictment of the teaching profession since there are many good reasons which give support to conventional morality. The school is an agent of socialization and part of its mandate is to help parents and society, in general, in the inculcation of conventional moral norms. These conventions are known as the collective wisdom which all new teachers need in order to get by and succeed in their task. We conjecture from limited data that a predominance of the number of teachers remain for the most part in the conventional stages (Stages 3 and 4) of morality.

Specific to our discussion is the teacher's level or stage of moral development in the classroom where moral and ethical issues are being discussed. Our own conviction is that it is important to have teachers at a post-conventional level of morality, in order to be able to help the class reflect on conventional moral norms and also to help in the process of generating new kinds of norms where necessary. This does not necessarily make the teacher a moral rebel or a danger to school order. In most instances post-conventional moral arguments recognize the need for conventions but they base the merits of the conventions on sound reasoning rather than on some unquestioned authority source. There are also discussions on contemporary social issues which will take students and the teacher into areas where there are no clear authoritative sources. The teacher must indicate to the student his own fallibility on matters such as these, if and when they arise in a classroom discussion. It would seem difficult for Stage four conventional "law and order" teachers to put themselves in this kind of a role because there will be a latent fear that if the teacher does not have all the answers, his classroom authority will be relinquished. Since the structure of the class usually leaves the teacher in a controlling position, he is typically the initial modulator of the level of the classroom discussion. If the teacher's emphasis is on the maintenance of "law and order" and "authority," the discussion is not likely to venture into levels where authority is questioned on rational grounds. To break this kind of set in teacher training will be no easy task. If we look back on our practicum we could see that teachers quite unconsciously fell into teacher-centered class formats even when they thought they were avoiding it. It will be very important in the future to help generate environments other than the teacher-centered format to alleviate some of the problems that moral indoctrination presents (Hunt and Sullivan, 1973).

It will also be important for psychologists and other social scientists to be sensitive to how their theories and findings are used in teacher training colleges. One example will suffice using Kohl-

berg's stage theory. It may occur as it did in our work with teachers, that they are interested in the moral development stages à la
Kohlberg. The question that educational psychologists must ask is
whether the psychological characteristic as it is described will have
effects on a teacher's attitude which may be detrimental. For example, by telling a teacher that one child is at an "instrumental
hedonist" stage, while another is at the "good boy—nice girl"
stage, does he run the risk of having the teacher negatively evaluate one stage over another in a stereotype rather than taking a developmental perspective? It seems that this is not a rare occurrence
and we are increasingly becoming aware of the moral issues that it
creates for social scientists when they give out to the public personality labels (see especially Rosenthal, 1971; Ryan, 1971). In one of
the schools in which we worked we inquired of the whereabouts of
a student in one of our bi-weekly classes and were told that the
teacher personally asked him to leave the class "because he was a
wise guy and a stage two." It is important to constantly be sensitive to the fact that the assessment instruments that we devise and
the labels we use can easily become tools of victimization by ourselves and the teachers with whom we work (Ryan, 1971).

c) *Specific Value Areas in the Curriculum*

We have indicated throughout this work that value education
pervades the whole school curriculum either implicitly or explicitly. At this point we would like to look a little more concretely at
the three most controversial value areas in education today,
morals, politics and religion. This will enable us to apply and elab-
orate some of the principles considered so far. We will first spend
some time discussing moral education, and then briefly compare
and contrast it with political and religious education.

Moral education is a sphere in which one gets into much more
immediate trouble by leading others astray than by going astray
oneself (Beck, 1974). At higher age levels, then, a teacher may
largely resolve the problem of legal sanctions by opting for a free
atmosphere and democratic procedures in the learning situations.
He can then express many of his own views and inject new ideas
into the discussion without being accused of *imposing* his ideas on
the students. And the students themselves may discuss and even

adopt quite extreme moral views with legal impunity. The views the teacher expresses must still be moderately sensible, for as a "model" to the young he is considered to be responsible even for his passing remarks. But no longer need he keep all or even most of his moral opinions to himself.

Legal culpability, however, is not our only concern. Some people in education (whether teachers, administrators, students) undoubtedly have an influence upon the moral development of others. To a degree, this is something over which they have no control. But given that morality is not merely "caught," the explicit statement of one's moral views, with supporting evidence and arguments, can increase considerably one's moral influence upon others. The question is, then: *should* we express our moral views even within the broad limits set by public sanctions?

The argument from controversy commonly given by philosophers against influential people in education expressing their moral views is as follows: since morality is a controversial area, in which we can never know who is right, it is irresponsible of us to influence someone else to accept our moral views, for they may be no sounder than the views he has already. However, in response to this argument, if we can never really know who is right, surely it does not matter whether we influence someone else morally or not. If our own views are just as likely to be right or wrong as the ones he has already (because the whole area is so controversial), it does not matter which views he ends up with. Of course, we may be wasting our time in trying to convince him, but that is comparatively weak objection. If moral discussion proves to be an enjoyable pastime—as most people find it—there can be no more objection to it than to watching football, which is also rather "a waste of time" but nevertheless enjoyable.

The argument from controversy, then, has to be modified somewhat. The point, it may be conceded, is not that there is *nothing* to choose between different moral opinions; rather it is that there is not *enough* to choose between them. There is always so much uncertainty about moral matters—witness the controversy surrounding them—that even if our views are generally regarded as being rather sensible, we have no right to present them to students as if they had been established. As Bertrand Russell has said, the degree of conviction with which we hold to our beliefs should be no greater than the extent of the evidence for them.

Now, however, we have an argument not against moral education in general, but against moral education carried on in a particular way, namely, by means of dogmatic instruction. And while the argument is overstated, it is one that in broad outline we might accept. It has been put more reasonably, for example, by John Wilson (1961), who says that "religious, political and moral beliefs are *uncertain*, in a sense in which mathematics and Latin grammar are not uncertain. And . . . we object to closing people's minds on uncertain issues. . . . We must grade our teaching to fit the logical status of the beliefs which we are putting forward. If they are certain . . . they can be taught as certainties: if they are merely probable . . . they must be taught as probabilities. . . ." This seems to make good sense, and to accord with the free, critical approach to learning we have been advocating. There is no room in educational institutions for people who impose their views on others on the basis of conferred status alone, regardless of considerations of evidence and probability. In free, cooperative inquiry, sharing of beliefs naturally includes sharing information concerning the extent of the evidence for the beliefs.

We must be careful, however, not to overstate the degree of controversy and uncertainty that exists in moral matters. Is it wrong to kill people? Is it good to be kind to people? In certain types of situations, for certain types of people, the answer very obviously is *yes*. There is an enormous amount of agreement around the world on moral matters, as Morris Ginsberg has shown very clearly, and there is no reason to believe that this is simply a matter of everyone making the same mistakes (Ginsberg, 1956). Often we fail to see the extent of the agreement because we do not notice relevant differences in circumstances that require the drawing of different moral conclusions from the same principles. In some cases for example, it may not be good to be kind to people, but then there will be exceptional circumstances that most people would see as justifying a different course of action. Further, we are often so impressed by the multiplicity of moral views on a particular matter that we fail to consider whether they might not all represent equally good means to the same ends; or, if not equally good, at least all considerably superior to other alternatives one might adopt if one did not apply oneself to the sound solution of moral problems (Beck, 1974).

In physics, we do not rest easily with two equally adequate but differing solutions to the same problem, for our immediate concern is not a practical one. We wish to find out what is *the explanation* of a set of phenomena. But in morals (and physical engineering) it is different. We may hit upon a solution to a particular practical problem, refine it using a number of *ad hoc* techniques, and then set about implementing it without paying much attention to the question *why* this solution happens to work. Of course, a mature moral science must include a comprehensive investigation of "why" questions, for in the long run that will bear a great deal of practical fruit. But at least as much time will always be spent on the development and application of short-term problem solving techniques, for there will always be pressing, immediate needs. (Perhaps physics, too, should be more practically oriented: but that is another issue.) (Beck, 1974.)

In morals, then, the crucial question is not what is *the* right solution, but what is a good solution. For this reason a wide variety of solutions can reasonably be tolerated. A particular group of students, however, can profitably get together and work out a solution to a problem that concerns them. The other side of the principle that a number of solutions will do is that a group of people can decide that *they* will tackle the problem in a particular way. Further, insofar as different students *must* adopt different solutions because of their circumstances, they can still share insights into ultimate life goals, general moral principles, and the methodology of moral inquiry. They can even make constructive criticisms of each other's solutions, without necessarily accepting them for themselves.

It is clearly a mistake, then, to rule out moral education on the ground that morality is a controversial area. And if we review attempts that have been made to do so, we find that a strong supplementary (though often unconscious) reason has been to preserve a specific set of moral values that are held to be objectively valid and indeed beyond question. Paradoxically, extreme relativism has been an ally of extreme objectivism. Moral discussion is kept out of the school because there are no answers, but also because we already know the answers and do not want immature minds questioning them. This is not such a paradox as it may seem, of course, for acceptance of the dogmatic mode of moralizing involves acceptance of a babel of conflicting and irreconcilable dogmas, which is what has done so much to give morals the name of a "controversial area."

There is room for fundamental and ineliminable differences in value orientation, such that there is no higher criterion according to which one orientation can be said to be better than another. However, recognition of this fact, far from increasing the air of controversy surrounding morals would overcome a whole range of controversies, in areas where people do not disagree but are simply different. It would then be possible to concentrate effort upon the areas of real disagreement that do exist.

Many of the methods of moral education developed in recent years—the skills approach, the value clarification approach, the case study approach, the Kohlberg "stimulation of natural development" approach—have been attempts to get around the problem of the controversial nature of moral questions, to avoid indoctrination in an area in which, it has been thought, to say anything of a substantive nature is to indoctrinate. Our claim is that morals is like any other area of inquiry in that some answers are better than others, and a teacher or student can contribute to the finding of better answers by saying what he thinks and why. Hence, while these more detached procedures for moral education do provide useful supplementary techniques, they neglect one of the central activities of moral education: the cooperative development of a body of sound, substantive moral ideas.

Turning to political education, we find that many similar remarks can be made. Teachers have been shunted out of political education, partly on the ground that politics cannot be handled in an objective, rational manner like other school subjects—it is too controversial—and partly in order to protect sacred political assumptions that are taken for granted in the school. A certain amount of detached study *about* politics and political ideas is possible within the traditions of political history and political science. But it would be entirely inappropriate to tackle head-on and in a spirit of genuine inquiry the question whether, for example, democracy really is better than communism.

Once again, a teacher can protect himself legally and professionally by encouraging democratic learning procedures, but that is not really the point. For so long as we continue to accept the notion that politics is merely a matter of opinion, in which the cooperative development of a body of sound attitudes and beliefs on substantive issues is impossible, the study of politics will go badly. We must learn how to sort out the various types of problems within the political sphere, determine the methodology appropriate to each, and calmly set about finding more adequate solutions to these problems. We must not, of course, exaggerate the strength of our arguments or the weight of our evidence. But equally we must not go to the other extreme and assume that neither arguments nor evidence can ever show one political procedure or arrangement to be better than another (Beck, 1974).

In politics, even more than in morals, there has been a tendency to assume that ideas, attitudes and principles necessarily come in systems, and one must accept or reject the whole ideological package. This has increased the impression of disagreement and controversy, for people have been discouraged from noticing common features in different political systems. It has also confirmed the belief that ordered political inquiry is impossible, for we have been prevented from noticing the many examples of political procedures and arrangements, arrived at on the basis of experience and thought, that are almost universally considered to be sound (in practice if not in ideology). A first step in restoring political education to its proper place would be to conceptualize the issues less in terms of total systems and more in terms of specific (though interrelated) political principles and strategies. This also would have the very practical advantage that students with rather different political orientations and needs could work together on particular problems. Principles for reducing inefficiency in bureaucracies, for example, may be studied with equal interest by two students who differ considerably on the issue of socialistic equalization.

Political and moral education are very closely related. People who have advocated traditional "character formation" through the school have often been opposed to political education. But effective political education is an essential concomitant of moral education, properly understood. For in a great many moral situations a person cannot act wisely or effectively if he is not familiar with the wider societal context and consequences of this action. Further, enormous transfer can be achieved from political education to moral education, for both are concerned with identifying ultimate life goals, with harmonizing the pursuits of different individuals and groups, and with developing strategies for the achievement of goals (Beck, 1974).

Religion as a so-called controversial area may appear at first glance to present quite a different set of tasks for education than morals and politics; but in fact a number of similarities can be traced. To begin with, the false opposition of total religious systems, parallel to the opposition of political systems, can and must be overcome. Common attitudes to life, to other people, to the world, to the deity (or deities) can be found within different religions. It has been customary for the exponents of particular religions to play down these common elements in order to establish the distinctiveness and superiority of their own religion; but this is a propagandistic trick that can no longer be tolerated. Either a particular religion is distinctive and superior or it is not, and insofar as it is not, this fact must be admitted (and even, perhaps, made an object of celebration).

Further, it is becoming increasingly apparent that religions have common elements for good reason: they serve similar functions in the lives of individuals and groups. And once this is recognized, the possibility of cooperative, ordered inquiry into religious issues and practices is opened up, just as in morality and politics. Such inquiry must not disregard general principles of experience, evidence and reasonableness. But provided it does not, there are no grounds for excluding the study and experience of religion from a comprehensive program of open education in which people are free to state their views and the reasons for them (Beck, 1974).

There is a particular need for religion-like perspectives in education at the present time. After an era of extreme specialization and compartmentalization in human activities and inquiries, we are lacking in the kind of overviews that a religion (or a metaphysics) can give. Even ethics, which is relatively broad in scope, tends to concentrate on value questions. There is need for a comprehensive treatment of such questions as the nature of man, the nature of experience, the nature of existence, the meaning of life. These are touched on, of course, in a great many separate disciplines, but the findings of these disciplines must constantly be brought together into a rigorous, creative and useful set of outlooks, attitudes and principles.

We are not suggesting that questions such as whether there is a God or whether there is life after death are not controversial. But the point is that to a large extent they have been artificially *made* controversial by religious leaders who force people to take a stand on them. Without this element of compulsion, they could be incorporated into an education program as topics of experience and serious study. Further, they could be opened up for reinterpretation by people who do not accept an affirmative answer in any literal sense but who might benefit enormously from their associated spiritual and metaphysical meanings. Like moral and political questions, they could be rendered manageable if we did not assume beforehand that they are meaningless, or that they are just a matter of opinion, or that the answers are so clear that we must not muddy the waters by allowing students to inquire into them (Beck, 1974).

In this section we have reiterated that the fact that an area is controversial is no reason not to study it. A great deal of worthwhile study can be carried out in controversial areas such as morals, politics and religion. But this is to take a rather negative, defensive position. We would like to close the section by putting the point more positively and more strongly. It seems to us that, far from keeping controversial areas out of education, they should be given the major part of our attention. This does not necessarily mean that they should be added as new "subjects," for we must move away from a traditional "subject" orientation in all problem areas. But, on the average, people in educational institutions should spend well over half of their time grappling with issues that are centrally or almost centrally concerned with so-called controversial areas such as morals, politics and religion. This is necessary, if education is to be restored to a proper place in society and in our lives.

d) *The Relation between School and Community in the Wider Moral Perspective*

We might note, finally, that education itself is emerging as a major controversial area that cannot any longer be kept out of the curriculum of educational institutions. It is akin to morals and politics and should, by the same arguments, be open to free, frank discussion by teachers and students. This is implicit, of course, in any proposals for democratic decision-making in educational institutions. For if students are to be involved in educational decisions, they must spend a considerable amount of time inquiring into how education should be carried on (Beck, 1974).

Such questioning of the nature and aims of education has tended to be suppressed in the past, perhaps in the belief that discipline would be difficult to maintain and pursuit of the prescribed goals might slacken once students became self-conscious and critical about what was happening to them. But this implies that teachers or other authorities always know best what is good for students, an assumption that must be questioned. Further, it shows an excessive pessimism about human nature: why should people stop doing something, even if it involves considerable effort at times, simply because they become aware of what they are doing and why? And further, it overlooks entirely the principle that people tend on the whole to attain goals more effectively when they are aiming at them than when they are not. To fail to enlist the conscious involvement of students in the planning of their own education is, when one thinks about it, the height of absurdity.

Some people attack democratic decision-making in educational institutions on the ground that precious time is being taken away from the very activity for which the institution exists: namely, education. But this raises an entirely false distinction between engaging in an activity and making the decisions that guide that activity from day to day. It is like distinguishing between driving a car and deciding where to position it from moment to moment on the road. The parallel objection would be that one is taking time out of driving in order to decide which way to turn the steering wheel. Obviously, giving attention to questions about the nature and aims of education is an integral part of gaining an education.

It is remarkable how far up the formal educational ladder this reluctance to let students seriously discuss education goes. Even in graduate school, where teachers and students are sometimes separated only by a year of studies and a degree-conferring ceremony, the issues of education are seldom raised. The ultimate anomaly is found in the graduate school of education, where professors advocate the implementation of progressive programs in schools while refusing to participate with their own students in the thorough assessment, and, as appropriate, revision of their current educational experiences. Sometimes, indeed, the situation is much more oppressive at the graduate school level, because of a more direct link between pleasing one's teacher and having good occupational prospects after graduation (Beck, 1974).

More specific to our present discussion is the school in the wider community context. We have suggested elsewhere (Beck, 1971) that more adequate studies of values could begin immediately within the present curriculum structure, "organically fused" with the current activities of existing school departments. A committee of consultants, teachers, students, *and others* could draw up lists of topics, and these could be spread appropriately around a school so that an interdepartmental program involving all age groups might be developed. The time has come to look more closely at the input of the "and others" group—notably parents and other community members—and consider generally the role of the community in moral education.

At the outset, we must acknowledge that there are other moral education agencies in the community in addition to the school. The family is of great importance, especially because of its crucial effect upon the child during the first few years of life. Various religious organizations also play a major role, directly through their moral education programs and public stance and indirectly through their influence upon parents who in turn are to influence children. Television, radio, cinema, books, and so on obviously are a significant factor. And major institutions in the community from the law court to the factory have an effect upon people's moral thought and behavior through the principles they espouse, the practices they adopt and the pressures they exert upon people.

The present work concentrates on the role of the *school* in moral education, and in this section upon the part the community can play in assisting the *school*. But it is important for us to keep in mind the influence of other agencies of the kind just mentioned, for a school program must enlist their aid if it is to be successful. From a negative point of view, the work of the school will be constantly frustrated if the value beliefs and attitudes developed there are at variance with the ones being learned in the rest of the community. Looking at the matter positively, the school will be able to achieve much more if its work is part of a total community program of moral education and reform.

Community reform is as important as community moral education. In the schools it is being recognized increasingly that moral education can be really effective only if the organizational structure and human relationships in the school match the moral principles and reasoning procedures being learned. For example, it is virtually impossible to learn post-conventional, reflective morality in an authoritarian classroom. And the same is true in the community. A thoughtful, tolerant outlook in moral matters cannot easily be developed in a community where the various institutions—family, organized religion, the law, politics, the civil service, business houses, factories—require unthinking obedience to arbitrarily imposed rules and arbitrarily appointed authorities. The reappraisal of our way of life—including our institutional way of life—that is going on in the schools must be linked with a total reappraisal throughout the community. We must all work together on improving the quality of life in our society if we are to develop morally.

In saying this, we do not wish to suggest that there are easy solutions. For example, we do not see any value in an immediate abandonment of all rules and authority structures. It seems to us that our society is characterized by too much authority in some areas and not enough in others (Beck, 1974). We must not do away with rules and authority structures, but rather develop a more informed, reflective, selective, creative approach to them: the post-conventional approach advocated in *Moral Education in the Schools*. There is much that is good in the moral rules and institutional structures existing in our communities at present, and we must conserve this element as we introduce modifications and additions. However, because there are no easy solutions, that is all the more reason for involving the whole community in moral reform. Moral education cannot be merely something that we employ teachers to do for our children, so that an educational institution is a kind of moral finishing school, initiating the young into established moral traditions. Moral education and moral creation is something we must all be involved in from day to day throughout our lives. Adults and children must progress together and learn together.

Members of the community have both an "interest input" and an "insight input" into moral education in the schools. Whether as parents or as ordinary citizens they have a stake in what kind of young people emerge from the school experience: it will affect their own lives directly and also the well-being of their community as a whole. Accordingly, they have a right to influence the schools to some extent along the lines of their own self-interest. Equally, they should play a part in program planning in the school because of their distinctive insights into what is needed and how it can best be achieved. They have a longer experience of life than school students, and often a broader perspective than professional educators. Of course, there is no question of absolute control by external community members of what goes on in schools: what is needed is a team relationship between students, professional educators and community members. However, community members must have a major voice in what is done, and not simply be asked for advice that is then either accepted or ignored. Their role must be participatory and not merely consultative.

In determining community representation on committees making decisions about moral education programs, we should not be concerned with numbers alone. Even if half the members of a committee are from outside the school, this does not ensure that "the community" is adequately represented, for they may all be from one sector or stratum of the community. We must avoid the "prominent citizens" approach, and try rather to achieve representation from many different walks of life. Further, we must not fall into the trap of having heads of a great many organizations as *ex officio* members of the committee, for they will often be too busy to make an adequate input and will tend to have a uniform out-

look: that of heads of organizations. The aim should be to achieve
a high degree and wide diversity of interest input and insight input.
Nomination and election procedures must be developed to achieve
this end.

From within the schools, there should be strong representation from the students themselves with probably at least as many
students as professional educators on the decision-making body.
Once again, the twofold principle applies: the student body is a
highly interested party, since it is they who are to "undergo" the
educational experiences that are planned. And equally they have a
major insight input to make, since they have considerable awareness of the moral problems that confront them and also of the
learning methods that are most effective. Of course, the students
will have a "second chance": any sound program of moral education will allow considerable room for individual initiative and option on the part of students. But the activity of planning and guiding a program does set certain broad limits on what is to be
experienced and hence student participation is essential at this
level.

It is impossible to lay down a general formula for the com-
position and mode of operation of a community moral education
committee. Perhaps about one third of the members should be external community members, another third students and the re-
mainder professional educators and consultants. And perhaps the
group should meet frequently at the outset to recommend general
programs for the schools and then less frequently to guide implementation and introduce modifications. But different arrangements will be found appropriate for different schools or school districts. For example, a spontaneous experiment in moral education
conducted by members of a particular school may provide the
focal point for initial deliberations and decisions. Or it may be
thought advisable to establish a few broad guidelines, call for program proposals from the schools, and then proceed further in the
light of the ideas that emerge. It is often best to begin immediately
with some activities and modify them as one goes along, rather
than deliberate for a couple of years without adequate practical experience and then propose a total package that may prove to be

unusable. We all have a few ideas before we begin and we will never have all the answers, no matter how long we deliberate.

Beck (1971) has recommended for immediate implementation the kind of interdepartmental study of values outlined very broadly on pages 8 and 9 of *Moral Education in the Schools*. This plan, the details of which would have to be filled in by an appropriate body, has the advantage that it requires no new legislation with respect to schools and little institutional reorganization. It simply involves making explicit and coordinating a study of values that should already be going on in our schools. According to all the major statements of aims, formal education is intended to foster the development of character and sound values in students. By neglecting this aspect of education we have failed to live up to our basic expectations for schooling and, furthermore, have given students the impression that we do not consider values to be particularly important.

But is it really possible for a representative group of students, educators and community members to agree on a moral education program for the schools? It seems to us that it is possible, but as we enter upon the attempt, certain hard facts must be recognized. To begin with, moral education will always be surrounded by a certain amount of controversy. The crucial question is not whether we can arrive at a program that will make *everyone* entirely happy —for that is unlikely—but whether we can afford to go on neglecting value issues in the schools. We have avoided the serious discussion of values in the schools out of a perfectionist concern that no one should be offended. But the crisis of values in the world today has made it obvious that *some* solution, even if it is somewhat makeshift, must be developed in the area of values if the human race is to survive. Further, with the current talk of "deschooling society" and the growing criticism of so many school activities, it is apparent that there is no longer a large array of "clearly acceptable" school subjects to take precedence over the study of values.

Another and related hard fact that we must face is that programs in values and related subjects will often have to be brought in by majority vote, without the approval of every individual who has been involved in the discussions. For too long on education committees and school boards we have operated according to the gentlemanly principle that if a subject is controversial it should be dropped: unless complete consensus can be achieved, it would be bad form to proceed further. This simply leads to education at the level of the lowest common denominator or, if the decision-making committee is unrepresentative, to education according to the prejudices of a particular community sub-group. Certainly, we must strive for wide acceptability in value programs, grounded in the broadly beneficial nature of the proposals developed. But we must not be afraid to implement programs on the basis of majority opinion.

Of course, there is a large corpus of democratic theory concerned with the protection of individual or minority rights against tyranny of the majority. This theory should be further developed and applied to the problems of education in controversial areas. One obvious safeguard, noted earlier, is to ensure that the individual student has considerable opportunity to choose his own learning activities. Attention should also be given to developing programs that are of substantial value to all parties, even though they are not *ideal* for all parties. It is often possible to hit upon "happy compromises" in curriculum planning if we work at it hard enough. In attempting to arrive at such compromises in the area of values, a key principle to bear in mind is that there are often many solutions to a given moral problem, all of which are considerably better than certain alternatives. Accordingly, a group of students can engage in moral education activities that each finds highly beneficial, even though they arrive at different solutions to the issues being faced. Perhaps some gain more from the program than others, but all benefit. It is programs of this kind that we must try to develop in the schools.

It might be thought that one could achieve community consensus with respect to moral education programs by concentrating on cases rather than issues, on methods rather than content, on comparative ethics rather than problem-centered ethics. But each of these approaches has been tried and found to be inadequate as *the* method of moral education (see Beck, 1974, Chapter 8). An approach that skirts around the issues inevitably fails to give very much help in dealing with the issues. Furthermore, as participants in the process of moral reform, community members cannot remain aloof from the substantive issues, and simply devise neat moral discussion games for their children to play at school. They will be concerned that certain issues are raised and considered very thoroughly at school, for they will see them to be of crucial importance for the children and for the community as a whole.

In order to achieve the kind of community involvement in moral education in the schools that we are proposing, it is clear that we must go beyond the initial decisions about the discussion topics, major issues, learning activities, coordinated programs, and teacher selection and in-service training. A total structure of *continuing* interaction between the school and the community in value areas must be established. To a large extent the present barriers between the school and the community must be broken down. There must be frequent opportunities for adult community members to share their concerns with groups of school students, and vice versa. Debate by the community about industrial projects, environmental problems, legal cases and the like must be deliberately and systematically carried into the schools. Debate by the schools about value issues must wherever possible be conducted in a relevant community context, with informed community members present to make a contribution. It is the resources of the community, and not merely its curriculum suggestions, that the schools so desperately need. Students should be able to participate in a genuine way in the institutions of the community so that there is a two-way process of assisting and learning. The community helps to find answers with respect to the nature of moral education programs; but to a considerable degree it is itself the problem, the object of study, and should be open to study and reform.

We are not suggesting, however, that the distinction between the school and the community be broken down entirely. Society should not be "deschooled", in one commonly understood sense of the word. There will always be a need for institutions that concentrate to a relatively high degree on learning, enabling people for a period to achieve a necessary distance from and perspective on the problems with which they are grappling. Rather, we are proposing that there be a constant and genuine interaction between the school and the community.

It might be thought that school administrators and teachers will feel threatened by the prospect of extensive community involvement in school decision-making. However, we cannot see why this should be the case, since in general the hand of the professional educator is strengthened if he can point to the fact that the programs in his school have community support. And this would be especially so in the case of a moral education program, where the very possibility of having such a program is clearly dependent upon some degree of approval from the community. Neglect of value issues in the schools has often been seen as a necessity on the ground that "we live in a pluralistic society" and any form of public education must avoid controversial issues. But if a group with broad community representation can arrive at agreement upon a moral education program, even if it represents something of a compromise, such arguments will fall to the ground.

It is true that in order to arrive at agreement, certain safeguards will have to be adopted, depending upon the particular concerns of the community in question. Selection of teachers and other resource people will have to take place according to procedures that ensure that all major viewpoints are adequately represented. Certain issues will have to be dealt with at a relatively general level in order to protect the feelings of particular individuals or minority groups. Some topics may have to be avoided completely, at least for a period, because they are too emotional or controversial to permit fruitful discussion. But there is good reason to believe that precautions of this kind can be taken without in any way undermining the value of a moral education program. And the overwhelming advantage will be that a program will emerge that can be implemented with community understanding, cooperation and support.

References

Ausubel, D.P. and Sullivan, E.V. *Theory and problems of child development*, (2nd Ed.). New York: Grune & Stratton, 1970.

Beck, C.M. Moral education in the schools: Some practical suggestions. *Profiles of Practical Education*, No. 3. Toronto: The Ontario Institute for Studies in Education, 1971.

Beck, C.M. *Ethics: An introduction*. Toronto: McGraw-Hill, Ryerson, Ltd., 1972.

Beck, C. *Education philosophy and theory: An introduction*. Boston: Little Brown, 1974.

Beck, C.M., Crittenden, B.S. and Sullivan, E.V. (Eds.). *Moral education: Interdisciplinary approaches*. Toronto: University of Toronto Press, New York: Newman Press, 1971.

Beck, C.M., Sullivan, E.V. and Taylor, N. Stimulating transition to post-conventional morality: The Pickering High School Study. *Interchange*, *3*(4), 1972, 28-37.

Crittenden, B. *Form and content in moral education*. Monograph Series, No. 12. Toronto: The Ontario Institute for Studies in Education, 1972.

Crittenden, B. *Education and social ideals: A study in philosophy of education*. Toronto: Longman Canada Ltd., 1973.

Dewey, J. *Moral principles in education (1909)*. New York: Philosophical Library, 1959.

Ginsberg, M. On the diversity of morals. In his collection *On the Diversity of Morals*. London: Heinemann, 1956, Chapter VII.

Girvetz, H.K. (Ed.). *Contemporary moral issues*, (2nd Ed.). Belmont, California: Wadsworth Publishing Company, Inc., 1968.

Hare, R.M. Adolescents into adults. In T.H.B. Hollins (Ed.), *Aims in Education: The Philosophical Approach*. England: U. of Manchester Press, 1964.

Hunt, D. and Sullivan, E.V. *Between psychology and education*. Chicago: Dryden Press, 1973.

Jackson, P.W. *Life in the classroom*. New York: Holt, Rinehart and Winston, 1968.

Kohlberg, L. Stages of moral development as the basis for moral education. In C.M. Beck, B.S. Crittenden and E.V. Sullivan (Eds.), *Moral Education: Interdisciplinary Approaches*, Chapter I. Toronto: University of Toronto Press, New York: Newman Press, 1971.

Morris, W. Indoctrination as a normative concept. S.P.E., Vol. 4, Summer, 1966.

Murdoch, I. Metaphysics and ethics. In D.F. Pears (Ed.), *The Nature of Metaphysics*. New York: Macmillan Ltd., 1962, 99-123.

Peters, R.S. A plea for pluralism. In Theodore Mischel (Ed.), *Cognitive Development and Epistemology*. New York: Academic Press, 1971.

Piaget, J. *Insight and illusions of philosophy*. New York: The World Publishing Co., 1971.

Porter, N. and Taylor, N. How to assess the moral reasoning of students: A teacher's guide to the use of Lawrence Kohlberg's stage-developmental method. *Profiles of Practical Education*, No. 8. Toronto: The Ontario Institute for Studies in Education, 1972.

Report of the Committee on Religious Education in the Public Schools of the Province of Ontario. Toronto: Ontario Department of Education, 1969.

Rosenthal, R. Teacher expectations and their effects upon children. In G.S. Lesser (Ed.), *Psychology and Educational Practice*. Glenview, Illinois: Scott Foresman, 1971, 64-89.

Ryan, W. *Blaming the victim*. New York: Vintage Books, paperback, 1971.

Sullivan, E.V. Piagetian theory in the educational milieu: A critical appraisal. *Canadian Journal of Behavioral Science*, 1969, *1*, 129-155.

Sullivan, E.V. Piaget and the school curriculum: A critical appraisal. Toronto: The Ontario Institute for Studies in Education, Bulletin, No. 2, 1967.

Sullivan, E.V. and Beck, C.M. Moral education. In N. Bryne and J. Quarter (Eds.), *Must Schools Fail?: The Growing Debate in Canadian Education*. Toronto: McClelland and Stuart Ltd., 1972, 126-141.

Sullivan, E.V., McCullough, G. and Stager, M. A developmental study of the relationship between conceptual, ego and moral development. *Child Development*, 1970, *41*(2), 399-411.

Tate, G. On indoctrination. Toronto: The Ontario Institute for Studies in Education. Unpublished paper, 1970.

Wilson, J. Education and indoctrination. In T.H.B. Hollins (Ed.), *Aims in Education: The Philosophical Approach*. Manchester England: U. of Manchester Press, 1964.

Wilson, J., Williams, N. and Sugarman, B. *Introduction to moral education*. United Kingdom: Penguin Books, 1967.